Acts of Implication

THE MRS. WILLIAM BECKMAN PROFESSORS

Department of English
University of California, Berkeley

1956–57	Harry Levin
1958–59	Stephen Spender
1960–61	Samuel Monk
1961–62	V. S. Pritchett
	Leo Marx
1962–63	Alfred Kazin
1963–64	Dwight MacDonald
1964–65	Maynard Mack
1965–66	Rossell Hope Robbins
1966–67	Noam Chomsky
	Joseph H. Summers
1967–68	Angus Wilson
1968–69	Northrop Frye
1969–70	L. C. Knights
	Gordon Ray
1970–71	Jean-Jacques Mayoux
1972–73	Robert M. Adams
1973–74	John Lehmann
	Frederick Dupee
1974–75	Richard Poirier
1975–76	Seamus Heaney
1977–78	Irvin Ehrenpreis
1978–79	Wayne C. Booth

ACTS *of* IMPLICATION

Suggestion and Covert Meaning
in the Works of
Dryden, Swift, Pope, and Austen

IRVIN EHRENPREIS

THE BECKMAN LECTURES • Berkeley, 1978

UNIVERSITY OF CALIFORNIA PRESS
Berkeley • Los Angeles • London

University of California Press
Berkeley and Los Angeles, California

University of California Press, Ltd.
London, England

© 1980 by
The Regents of the University of California

ISBN 0-520-04047-3
Library of Congress Catalog Number: 80-53161
Printed in the United States of America

1 2 3 4 5 6 7 8 9

To FREDSON THAYER BOWERS

καὶ τὰ λοιπά μου
μέλου δικαίως, ὥσπερ ἐς τόδ᾽ ἡμέρας

Contents

Acknowledgements and Short Titles

Unless otherwise indicated, I quote from the following editions:

Jane Austen, *Letters*, ed. R. W. Chapman, 2nd ed. (London and New York: Oxford University Press, 1952), cited as *Letters*.

———, *Novels*, ed. R. W. Chapman (Oxford: Clarendon Press, 1923), cited by titles of individual novels.

John Dryden, *Works*, ed. E. N. Hooker et al. (Berkeley and Los Angeles: University of California Press, 1956–), cited as *Works*.

Alexander Pope, *Correspondence*, ed. George Sherburn (Oxford: Clarendon Press, 1956), cited as *Correspondence*.

———, *Poems*, Twickenham Edition, ed. John Butt et al. (London: Methuen, 1939–69), cited as *Poems*.

Jonathan Swift, *Correspondence*, ed. Harold Williams (Oxford: Clarendon Press, 1963–65), cited as *Correspondence*.

———, *Drapier's Letters*, ed. Herbert Davis (Oxford: Clarendon Press, 1935), cited as *Drapier*.

———, *Poems*, ed. Harold Williams, 2nd ed. (Oxford: Clarendon Press, 1958), cited as *Poems*.

———, *Prose Works*, ed. Herbert Davis et al. (Oxford: Blackwell, 1939–68), cited as *Prose Works*.

In quoted passages I have freely altered the use of capitals, italics, and punctuation; and I indicate ellipses only within a quotation.

The chapter on Jane Austen appeared in a shortened form in the *New York Review of Books.*

I am deeply grateful to the Department of English of the University of California at Berkeley for inviting me to deliver the Beckman Lectures for 1978, on which these essays are based.

Introduction

i

To anyone who reads these essays, it will be obvious that the arguments rest on a central principle of judgment and interpretation; I assume that for most literature produced more than a hundred years ago, the aesthetic value is best approached by way of the meaning—i.e., that meaning, implicit, plain, or explicit, which the author invites the reader to share with him.[1] "Es gibt kein Verstehen ohne Wertgefühl," says Dilthey; but the maxim may be reversed.[2]

In this spirit I have tried to survey methods of implying or suggesting meaning in literary works attached to a tradition loosely named Augustan. Critics often talk as if English authors of the period 1660–1820 who are morally didactic and who strive for an air of clarity cannot also imply meanings with the utmost subtlety. Or they talk as if implication and covert meaning, to interest us, have to disagree with the more open pronouncements of an author.

1. Generally, in my use of "meaning" and "implication," I follow the analysis of E. D. Hirsch in *Validity in Interpretation* (New Haven: Yale University Press, 1967), pp. 49–51, 61–67, 89–102.
2. Wilhelm Dilthey, "Die Entstehung der Hermeneutik," *Gesammelte Schriften* (Stuttgart: Teubner, 1957), V, 336.

I wish to show that subtlety and indirection do not by their nature work against didacticism or an apparently lucid style. To illustrate generic differences within the common techniques, I have chosen a playwright, an essayist, a poet, and a novelist. I assume throughout that in all genres certain themes (politics, religion, sexual passion) are more likely to call for implication than others. I also assume that authors normally indicate their views on such themes by the moral judgments they implicitly pass on the people (real or fictitious) who figure in their stories or expositions. So the concept of heroism naturally becomes a focus for the elaboration of the themes.

If four such different authors can fit inside the same program, one reason is that they share an acquiescent view of the social order and a distrust of courtiers and of courtly aristocrats. Dryden arrived at this outlook after the Glorious Revolution. But in his earlier, heroic plays, I think one may find him already uneasy with the notions of heroism expected by the court that patronized him. Near the end of his career, in the poem addressed to his cousin, John Driden of Chesterton, he sketched a social and political philosophy which was, I believe, more natural to him, and the lineaments of which can still be traced in the novels of Austen. Swift mouthed a reverence for the crown, the court, and the aristocracy while his friends directed the government of England. But after they fell, his intuitive suspicion of unearned power displayed itself in his greatest works. Although Pope flirted with courtliness in *Windsor Forest*, his mature poems glisten with political alienation and scorn for the highest social classes.

In dealing with English literature of the period 1660–1820, therefore, a critic can discover general grounds for drawing out the covert or indirect meanings of accomplished authors. The institutions which provide the closest context of high literary functions are social. For artists and audiences of the years I survey, the theory or myth of a social hierarchy which was rational and enduring remained central to a view of the common weal. At first, the reaction against civil war, then the threat of

Jacobitism, then the expansion of industry and trade during a series of imperialist wars, turned intellectual effort away from disruptive speculations about the social organism. The cause of national unity against enemies like Jacobitism, France and Popery, or France and revolution discouraged the promoters of constitutional reform. Men like Mandeville, Wilkes, Fox, and Godwin did not unite behind them the section of the people that supplied the creators and patrons of imaginative literature.

In religious doctrine, during these years, the community of the Established Church softened its challenge to Dissent until specific articles of faith had little bearing on the religious principles of the literary population. "I am by no means convinced that we ought not all to be Evangelicals," said Austen.[3] Swift's venom against Presbyterianism, Fielding's distrust of Methodism, Scott's sympathetic critique of both Roman Catholicism and the narrowness of the Covenanters, Coleridge's doubts about the divinity of Christ, represent stages illustrating a gradual expansion of the idea of Christianity for those who delighted in poems, novels, and plays. But attitudes toward coarseness and obscenity remained stable.

In all genres the virtues of the hero of romance—honor, physical courage, the exaltation of personal fame over the common weal—gave way to varieties of Christian morality. Even more important, the ideal of the landed country gentleman as the exemplary social type persisted in the literary imagination.

With such common elements in mind I suggest that the ideological context within which poetic implication[4] does its main work was easy to define from the accession of Charles II to the death of George III. Even after we establish that context, some critics doubt that interpretations can be valid without reference to the individual interpreter. But I believe we can arrive at sound interpretations if we keep inside a proper frame-

3. *Letters*, ed. R. W. Chapman, 2nd ed. (London and New York: Oxford University Press, 1952), p. 410.
4. I use "poetry" in the sense of imaginative literature, whether prose or verse, lyric or epic, drama or novel.

work and limit our terms. Instead of seeking to demonstrate my case to all nations in all ages of the world, I wish to persuade listeners who already care about the free aesthetic experience of literature and who have a fair knowledge of works in various genres produced during the centuries from Chaucer to Tennyson.

I also take a narrow view of the terms "imply" and "implication." It is easy but dangerous to assume that polarities in literary terminology refer to mutually exclusive divisions which encompass the whole of a literary realm. If we employ words like "explicit" and "implicit," or "statement" and "suggestion," a reader may suppose that all discourse must belong to one or the other department.

Actually, however, most discourse is neither explicit nor implicit. The speech of an author cannot belong to either of these categories unless he seems aware of the fact. We do not apply the terms "implicit" and "explicit" to apparently unintentional effects. To be more precise, I suggest that in most speech we do not consciously or deliberately either speak out or veil our meaning. We merely say what we have to say in a context that supports, directs, and limits meaning. Between the two extremes of "implicit" and "explicit" lies a broad zone of speech that does not pretend to be deliberate.

If I seem confident in elucidating the works I examine, one reason is that I conceive of my problem not in terms of a general theory of hermeneutics but as centered on particular acts of literary interpretation. These acts take place between a speaker and a listener preoccupied with meanings controlled by art. One of the skills of literary genius is finding verbal equivalents for the gestures or vocal emphases which frame or focus acts of implication in conversation. Poetry differs from talk, confession, psychoanalytical sessions, etc., in that its meaning cannot be verified by spontaneous self-correction or impromptu cross-questioning in response to immediate evidence of misconstruction.[5]

5. Cf. Roman Jakobson on everyday phatic function and metalan-

Here, like most analysts of artful implication, I do not start from an infinite number of possibilities. In normal acts of literary interpretation we select one alternative from among several —often only two. Is Defoe ironical (we ask), in a scene from *Moll Flanders*, or is he not? The question we ask is seldom which is the perfect and irrefutable interpretation but rather which of two interpretations is the more probable. Now the choice among two, three, or four interpretations can be argued more convincingly than the absolute demonstration of a single one as quite perfect.

So also we do not address all possible listeners. In normal acts of interpretation we select an audience concerned with and prepared for the argument which we produce; and we judge that argument to be adequate if we can bring over this audience. When one claims that Austen implies a distrust of the peerage in *Mansfield Park*, one does not try to persuade listeners who have read no English novels of the nineteenth century. The chosen audience, to be persuaded of one out of two or three possible interpretations, constitutes a simpler, easier challenge than the human mind under the aspect of eternity searching for the absolutely true, undeniable explication of a crux in the Gospel according to St. John.

In choosing among several interpretations, I work from Dilthey's premise that context is normally the best guide—e.g., when one tries to decide whether or not a sentiment expressed by a character in Dryden's *Aureng-Zebe* is implicitly recommended by the play.[6] Sometimes, internal or rhetorical analysis can be determinate. Far more often, however, an interpretative critic sways his chosen audience by considering the actual,

guage: "Linguistics and Poetics," in T. A. Sebeok, ed., *Style in Language* (New York: Technology Press, 1960), pp. 355-56.

6. Dilthey, "Die Entstehung der Hermeneutik," p. 331. Cf. E. H. Gombrich, "The Priority of Context over Expression," in C. S. Singleton, ed., *Interpretation: Theory and Practice* (Baltimore: Johns Hopkins Press, 1969), pp. 68-104; also Gombrich, *In Search of Cultural History* (Oxford: Clarendon Press, 1969), passim. The example of *Aureng-Zebe* is of course my own.

shared world to which the literary work refers—perhaps by recalling the occasion which gave rise to the work, perhaps by sketching the circumstances which the work invites the reader to take for granted. It is largely by such means that one decides whether or not Swift was satirizing all "projectors" (i.e., all advocates of schemes for relieving human misery) in *A Modest Proposal*.

Finally, the drawing out of implications depends on imaginative sympathy. The listener must feel he can put himself in the place of the poet (known or unknown) as the subject of an imaginatively shared experience. He must, as Dilthey says, penetrate the inner creative process itself and then proceed to the outer and inner form of the literary work.[7] For example, when one elucidates a poem by Pope, one starts from a confidence that the author was supremely aware of the implications of his words, that he foresaw what readers might make of his innuendoes; the poet—we therefore feel—must have known that the audience of *The Dunciad* might associate the goddess Dulness with Queen Caroline herself as the corrupt zenith of a corrupt civilization. In drawing out the implications of Goldsmith's "The Traveller," one lacks such assurance.

Sympathetic penetration is a mystery, and can be an object of skepticism. Yet it is easy enough to defend. As Schleiermacher observed, we perform the act incessantly during routine communications with others, and human life would be impossible if we did not.[8] We verify the act by the consensus of our chosen audience—the person we are talking to, or the listeners whom we try to persuade of an interpretation. There is a mystery in one person's intuitively grasping what another means when he says, "I see something green," or "I am hungry," or in a woman's understanding of a child who complains, "I feel

7. *Selected Writings*, trans. and ed. H. P. Rickman (Cambridge, England: Cambridge University Press, 1976), p. 259.

8. "The Hermeneutics" (originally 1819), in *New Literary History* 10 (1979): 14–15.

lonely." These mysteries are no smaller than the leap of imagination demanded of us when Wordsworth or Stevens responds to a woman's song, or when T. S. Eliot responds to Sappho. For the purpose of establishing the context of meaning is, as Eliot says,

> not primarily that we should be able to think and feel, when reading the poetry, as a contemporary of the poet might have thought and felt, though such experience has its own value; it is rather to divest ourselves of the limitations of our own age, and the poet, whose work we are reading, of the limitations of *his* age, in order to get the direct experience, the immediate contact with his poetry.[9]

ii

The contrast between theory and practice calls for detailed examination. Scholars who wish to establish the general principles underlying the techniques of creative genius are ill-advised when they draw their evidence from the pronouncements of the artists without an exact analysis of their works. The practice of irony and satire is peculiarly subject to this caveat. Poets of the Restoration and the eighteenth century inherited a tradition of apologizing for satirical thrusts, and they invoked that tradition even when it was inappropriate. During the same period, a standard of lucidity existed which writers normally respected but which they also undermined, covertly, for special purposes.

Dryden liked to define "wit" as "a propriety of thoughts and words"[10]—i.e., lucidity and decorum combined. At least, this is how Swift enlarged a parallel definition: "When a man's thoughts are clear, the properest words will generally offer themselves first; and his own judgment will direct him in what order to place them, so as they may be best understood."[11] It

---

9. "The Frontiers of Criticism," penultimate paragraph, in *On Poetry and Poets* (New York: Farrar, Straus, and Cudahy, 1957), pp. 130–31.

10. "Apology for Heroic Poetry" and preface to *Albion and Albanius*, in *Essays*, ed. W. P. Ker (Oxford: Clarendon Press, 1900), I, 190, 270.

11. *Letter to a Young Gentleman*, in *Prose Works*, IX, 68.

is in fact fair to say that Lord Kames spoke for his age when he declared that "perspicuity ought not to be sacrificed to any other beauty whatever."[12]

If we doubted these witnesses, we should still find the authors themselves complaining that often when they tried to speak clearly, evil misinterpreters distorted their meaning. "Many an honest, well-meaning text has met with a wicked comment," said John Dennis.[13] In *An Essay on Criticism,* Pope echoed Dryden and Congreve, blaming those who, "*scandalously nice,* / Will needs *mistake* an author *into vice*" (ll. 556–57). The writer of *The Craftsman,* no. 2, remarked, "[No] man is safe against the subtleties and finesses of *lawyers* and *state chymists,* who can extract poison out of the most innocent things. . . . We have seen, in some reigns, *remote allegories, ironical expressions,* and the most *distant innuendo's* explain'd . . . to a man's destruction."[14] So also Gulliver cried out, in blazing innocence, to his cousin Sympson,

> [You said] that you were afraid of giving offence [i.e., by publishing *Gulliver's Travels*]; that people in power were very watchful over the press; and apt not only to interpret, but to punish every thing which looked like an *inuendo* (as I think you called it). But pray, how could that which I spoke so many years ago, and at above five thousand leagues distance, in another reign, be applyed to any of the Yahoos, who now are said to govern the herd. . . .[15]

The author of *The Doctrine of Innuendo's Discuss'd* registered a similar protest. Defending the transparently allusive and polemical history of England by "Mr. Oldcastle," he wrote:

> These remarks are laid down in such a plain and ingenuous manner, that one would imagine they could give no offence to

12. Henry Home, Lord Kames, *Elements of Criticism* (Edinburgh and London: A. Millar, 1762), II, 256 (chap. 18, sect. 2, para. 3).

13. *The Impartial Critick,* in *Critical Works,* ed. E. N. Hooker (Baltimore: Johns Hopkins Press, 1939), I, 31.

14. London, Dec. 12, 1726.

15. *Prose Works,* XI, 6.

any one; and as they are matters of fact extracted from the best historians, of things transacted some ages ago, how invidious is it in any man to wrest an author's meaning, and draw parallels where none were design'd?[16]

The Doctrine of Innuendo's Discuss'd is a whole pamphlet in which the author plays the game of pretending to be clear, candid, and straightforward while producing implicit condemnations of the persons he claims to be disregarding. His fundamental position is an irony much enjoyed by Swift and Pope:

> [That] a person entirely innocent of any crime should be ruffled at the mentioning of any villain who had happened ages before to be in the same post with himself, and construe every reflection upon him as a satyr upon himself, must seem very unaccountable to mankind, and make them imagine that he is conscious to himself of some secret guilt.[17]

Applying the supposed principle to Walpole, the author denies that "all the people in England" read the parallels and allegories of the opposition writers as allusions to the court:

> Did they [i.e., the ministerial spokesmen] ever consult all the people in England, to know in what sense they understood these papers? . . . Nay, were they ever inform'd that that *upright* and *incorrupt* gentleman, their patron, was imagin'd by the nation to be alluded to, whenever a Sejanus, a Wolsey, a Menzikoff, or a Cascia was mention'd? . . . For my part, I can't conceive how such an absurd notion could enter into their heads, as to think that a person of his uncommon abilities and integrity . . . could be designed under the characters which are the very reverse of him in every particular.[18]

Even the king and queen could be maligned by this trick; so the author laments that whenever *The Craftsman*, in citing passages from history,

> happens to mention a weak or bad prince, or a queen, it is unfairly and basely asserted by his antagonists that he alludes to

16. London, 1731, p. 6.   17. Ibid., pp. 7–8.
18. Ibid., pp. 13–14.

our most gracious sovereign and his consort. If this method of construction be allowed, what writer can be safe? [19]

Trustful moderns might presume, from such *cris de coeur*, that devious intentions were uncharacteristic of the eighteenth century.

Of course, the complaints authors made of being read wrong were often false, and the claim of lucidity was often a blind. Sometimes an essayist would pretend to be misunderstood in order to screen himself from punishment for having hurt the sensibilities of a great man. Sometimes a poet was jocular or sarcastic in his protests, teasing the reader into finding fresh innuendoes among the very disclaimers of old ones. We can learn a little about methods of implication by examining some particular examples of such devices and some general reflections on allegedly false reading. Even an informed modern critic does not always understand how self-conscious eighteenth-century writers were about their techniques of indirection.

In his "Apology" for *A Tale of a Tub*, Swift requested that his faults should not be "multiply'd by the ignorant, the unnatural, and uncharitable applications of those who have neither candor to suppose good meanings, nor palate to distinguish true ones." [20] As a clergyman (though anonymous) he protested furiously against the interpretations of three or four passages "which prejudiced or ignorant readers have drawn by great force to hint at ill meanings; as if they glanced at some tenets in religion"; and he insisted that he "never had it once in his thoughts that any thing he said would in the least be capable of such interpretations." [21] So he complained that irony had been mistaken for straightforward speech. [22]

Yet in the body of the *Tale* itself the author anticipated the perils he had finally to endure. "Nothing is more frequent," he said, "than for commentators to force [interpretations], which the author never meant." [23] Given such warnings, and accus-

---

19. Ibid., p. 11.
21. Ibid., p. 4.
23. Ibid., p. 118n.

20. *Prose Works*, I, 2.
22. Ibid.

tomed as one is to Swift's practice of subtlety and indirection, a critic must believe that Swift really hoped to shock readers by his rash language in the body of the *Tale*, but that he also refused to accept responsibility for his boldness. It is hardly credible that a man so deeply aware as Swift was, of the import that might be found in his words, would use dangerous expressions unwittingly.

Political themes fed the same equivocation as the religious themes. In the fifth *Drapier's Letter*, Swift declared bitterly that a judge had misinterpreted one of his essays as "reflecting" on George I and the royal ministers, and as trying to "alienate the affections" of the people of Ireland from those of England.[24] Yet we know that the Drapier was working toward precisely those ends, and that Swift simply dodged the legal consequences of his rhetoric.

Pope's work glitters with hypocritical complaints of being misunderstood. *The Dunciad* alone is a storehouse of specimens. Here when the poet describes his hero as supperless, a note reproaches "former commentators" for idly supposing that Cibber lacked a supper (I, 115). When the poem alludes to Hoadly's notorious sermon on "The Nature of the Kingdom of Christ," a note insists that the reference is to a "public orator," and not a clergyman (II, 368, in the 1729 edition). When a line implies that collaboration with Broome in translating the *Odyssey* was a painful ordeal, a note declares that the irony represents a "stroke" against Pope himself (III, 328, in the 1729 edition). Yet all of these together do not come up to the pseudonymous defense that Pope composed for his *Epistle to Burlington*. There he goes over the censorious, ironical lines following the denunciation of Timon's Villa—

> Yet hence the poor are cloath'd, the hungry fed;
> Health to himself, and to his infants bread
> The lab'rer bears: What his [i.e., Timon's] hard heart denies,
> His charitable vanity supplies—

24. *Drapier*, p. 101.

and interprets them not as accusing Timon's extravagant bad taste but as making an apology for it: " 'Tis an *innocent folly* and much more *beneficent* than the want of it," says the poet.[25] Clarity and explicitness were not the only virtues to which Pope aspired.

A special mark of the awareness these authors had of their indirections is the way they apologized for satires or censures that seemed to strike at identifiable individuals. (So-called "general" satire was commonly acceptable; "particular" was not.) As P. K. Elkin says, when authors of the late seventeenth and the eighteenth centuries wrote as critics, they advocated general satire; but when they were reproached for writing personal satire themselves, they felt obliged to offer a defense, "or to insist that they had been misinterpreted, that they had not for one moment intended slighting anyone in particular."[26] So also when an author used pseudonyms or initials for identifiable persons, "he could plead with some plausibility that he meant to hurt no one, and at the same time privately congratulate himself on having bagged . . . a brace of victims."[27]

Thus *The Craftsman*, no. 31, offers us two, mutually inconsistent replies to the charge of disingenuousness.[28] One defense is that the writer was being not devious but straightforward, in the passages singled out for condemnation. The other is that a political journalist must be devious when exposing the crimes of men in power.

So the Craftsman opens the topic by mentioning an objection to his style of blaming public officials, viz.

> that I am guilty of *disingenuity* and a *mean* design of calumniating men in high stations under *feigned characters*, and by other indirect methods, such as ironies, allegories, parallels, and remote *innuendoes*; which are called low arts. . . .

25. Pope, *Correspondence*, III, 255.
26. *The Augustan Defence of Satire* (Oxford: Clarendon Press, 1973), p. 139.
27. Ibid., p. 122.
28. London, Mar. 24, 1727.

The accusers (he reports) say that an honorable critic of the government would name his targets and produce verifiable evidence of misdoings. In reply, the Craftsman offers his pair of ill-matched statements. First he claims that in his discussions of politics he has no specific persons in mind. His aim is to "expose vice in general":

> But if two cases happen to be so much alike, that the generality of the world will compare what I relate of *former* times to the present; or any *great men* will apply bad characters to themselves, I do not think my self answerable for such *applications*. . . .

(Readers who take this remark seriously will not be challenged by me.)

Secondly, the Craftsman does not agree that one ought to accuse great men only in a judicial manner. When handling charges against private persons, the law—he says—can operate normally. But public figures resist the process:

> . . . *Great men* have frequent opportunities of *screening* themselves, in such a manner, by *cabals, alliances, corruption*, or the *favour* of an indulgent prince, that it is commonly very difficult to bring them to condign punishment, even when they are guilty of the most notorious oppressions, and are publicly complained of as the nuisances of their country.

Since everyone knew *The Craftsman* was established to oppose Walpole's government, and since the words "great" and "screen" were familiar expressions for the prime minister, an ironic innuendo is palpable here. But the general argument remains significant:

> [It] has always been a practice, under the most corrupt administrations, to quote *examples* and draw *parallels* out of history, in order to prove what effect the same male-practices have had on different states, or on the same states in former ages; nor can this be looked upon as *disingenuous* or a *libel* on the present *ministers* of any kingdom, any more than a comment on the ten commandments can be called a *libel* on every notorious sinner in the parish.

I grant, indeed, that it would be more honourable, as well as more *useful*, to write without *disguise*, provided it were equally *safe*. But would not any man be esteemed a *lunatick*, who should, in plain terms, attack such a monster as Wolsey or Buckingham, in the plenitude of their power; especially, if he has any *parallel instances* at hand, or can throw the same thoughts under *shades* and *allegories?*

About the time this number of *The Craftsman* appeared, Swift was composing similar remarks about an attack he had made on a dead judge who behaved himself unpatriotically and illegally. Some people, Swift said, thought the author had been too severe on the reputation of a man who after all was dead. The satirist replies to them with an argument like that of *The Craftsman*:

> What an encouragement to vice is this! If an ill man be alive and in power, we dare not attack him; and if he be weary of the world or of his own villainies, he has nothing to do but die, and then his reputation is safe. For these excellent casuists know just Latin enough to have heard a most foolish precept, that *de mortuis nil nisi bonum*; so that if Socrates and Anytus his accuser had happened to die together, the charity of survivors must either have obliged them to hold their peace or to fix the same character on both.[29]

Although it was conventional to declare that the only legitimate form of satire was general satire (i.e., attacks on types of men or kinds of vice, rather than on identifiable individuals), nevertheless, personal satire remained a common practice of disinterested writers; and their grounds for using it, as well as their methods of attack, were traceable to arguments like those offered by Swift.

So the place we arrive at seems almost an inversion of our first position. If clarity is accepted by one's readers as the mark of an excellent style, a subtle writer may convey eccentric meanings by affecting plainness and candor when he is in fact complex and indirect. The appeal to clarity then becomes a

29. Swift, *Prose Works*, XII, 24.

method of teasing the reader into thinking dangerously. As we have seen, a clever rhetorician will declare that obviously personal attacks are aimed at no individual, that thinly screened allusions are not allusions. After bringing out a passage that bristles with veiled, mutinous meaning (an allegory, a bit of parallel history), he may offer to explicate it, but then do so by giving an absurdly remote interpretation which still manages to point at the true sense.

A refinement of the scheme is a mock-defense. One opens with solemn, if misleading, apologies, supports these with unpersuasive reasons, and ends with a burlesque of the process of self-defense—in effect, showing off one's real animus. Thus Swift repudiates the view that Gay's fables point at living courtiers; but in developing his statement, he arrives at the ironic admission,

> [Although] it be highly probable, he [i.e., Gay] meant only the *courtiers* of former times, yet he acted unwarily, by not considering that the malignity of some people might misinterpret what he said, to the disadvantage of present *persons* and affairs.[30]

In the opposite way, a literary critic could deliberately miss the point of an allusive passage in order to insinuate the dullness of the author. Thus John Dennis has a long argument demonstrating that in *Prince Arthur*, Blackmore did not refer to William III. Of course, the poem is a transparent allegory of William's career; and Dennis is only concerned to reveal how badly the poet has misrepresented the character of the king.[31]

Craftsman 75 provides an elaborate instance of consciously false explication.[32] In an earlier paper the author had given an account of how "R——e" established himself as the corrupt governor of a city. Now the author proceeds to explain the dark story. To start, he discusses "allegories, allusions and fables,"

30. Ibid., p. 35.
31. Preface to *Remarks on Prince Arthur*, in *Critical Works*, I, 53–55.
32. London, Dec. 9, 1727.

and how "the learned" hide important meanings under such devices. He then moves on to an illuminating declaration:

> As therefore this *allegorical* way of writing is certainly the most *learned* as well as the most *antient*, so I hold it likewise to be the *safest* in all modern *performances*; especially if an author is, in any wise, addicted to writing on political *subjects*.

So he now undertakes to give the "whole meaning" of his allegory of the R——e.

In the explanation the Craftsman never mentions Walpole, who is certainly the "rogue" alluded to. Instead, he refers the allegory to the Knez Menzikoff (i.e., Alexander Menshikov, a favorite of Peter the Great, disgraced in 1727). Most people, he says, "discovered easily enough that the Knez Menzikoff was the person, whom I had in view; though possibly they might not understand every particular hidden stroke of satire that I intended." To elucidate these hidden strokes, he goes through the allegory of R——e point by point, treating each detail as an allusion to "the Knez Menzikoff," but employing expressions that direct us to Walpole. Once more, the pretence of lucidity has become a means of being covert and ambiguous.

So far from suffering unhappy misinterpretation, a polished writer could go even beyond the devices I have analyzed; for he could trick the reader into looking for secrets where there were none. Writing to Pope about the commentary on *The Dunciad*, Swift wondered whether the mock-editor should not "refine in many places, when you meant no refinement,"[33] and of course both *A Tale of a Tub* and *The Dunciad* exemplify this practice.

So also the ingenuity of the author could finally outrun the wit of even his most acute readers. Contemporary "keys" to *Gulliver's Travels* were inaccurate, clumsy, and dim-sighted. Swift in turn told Gay he had not realized that the quarrel between Peachum and Lockit in *The Beggar's Opera* alluded to the quarrel between Brutus and Cassius.[34] In an oft-quoted

33. Pope, *Correspondence*, II, 505.
34. Ibid., p. 482.

letter Swift told Pope that he found *The Dunciad* obscure: "I have long observ'd that twenty miles from London no body understands hints."[35] Meanwhile, his own French translator wrote to Swift that he had suppressed many of the allusions in *Gulliver's Travels* because "les allusions et les allégories, qui sont sensibles dans un pays, ne le sont dans un autre."[36] I have been dwelling on political implications. But sexual themes lead us to the same principles. Seldom indeed would an author admit pointblank that he had indulged in pornography. Wolseley was remarkable, in his encomiastic preface to Rochester's *Valentinian* (1685), for openly describing that noble author's obscene verses as indeed obscene.[37] The normal response to such a charge was to deny it, and to complain that the poet's sense had been distorted. Yet even while engaging in this ritual, the superior genius insinuated new improprieties.

One of the cleverest complaints is Wycherley's, in the dedication of *The Plain Dealer* (1677). The playwright scolds those who have discovered obscene innuendoes in *The Country Wife*. That he was perfectly serious one doubts. His real case is against persons proficient in finding and enjoying obscenity elsewhere and hypocritical in sounding disturbed by his comedy. He says that such readers "make nonsense of a poet's jest, rather than not make it bawdy."

A striking feature of Wycherley's discussion is the mixture of lubricity with wordplay. The dedication itself abounds in double meanings, many of them springing from the fact that the dedicatee was a procuress. Having started the infection, Wycherley soon makes it general. Innocent nouns and verbs are contaminated by their corrupt neighbors until the reader's mind exerts itself to invent pornographic hints. This stimulation of wordplay appears to be a special feature of sexual themes. Molière is remarkable for avoiding such wit, while his English imitators practice it.

35. Ibid., p. 504.
36. Swift, *Correspondence*, III, 217.
37. J. E. Spingarn, ed., *Critical Essays of the Seventeenth Century* (Oxford: Clarendon Press, 1908), III, 18–29.

With sexual themes, then, as with political and religious themes, writers often invited readers to expect an unorthodox or subversive meaning behind a veil of conventionality. And here too they seldom enjoyed being blamed for the accomplishment. When Jeremy Collier denounced Dryden for obscenity and profaneness, the victim said that he did retract all thoughts and expressions truly guilty of those faults. But he also declared that Collier, in many places, had "perverted my meaning by his glosses; and interpreted my words into blasphemy and bawdry, of which they were not guilty."[38] Yet the volume to which Dryden prefaced these remarks included not only "Sigismonda and Guiscardo" but also "Cinyras and Myrrha," in both of which the poet hardly restrained his knack for indecency.

Collier also drove Congreve into the task of defending himself against charges of obscenity and irreligion. In his reply Congreve complained of "malicious and strain'd interpretations." He blamed these upon Collier's own "impurity," and said the condemned passages only contracted their alleged filth by "passing thro' his very dirty hands." Where an expression itself was "unblameable in its own clear and genuine signification," said Congreve, Collier made it "bellow forth his own blasphemies."[39]

It is true that Collier regularly exaggerated the bawdiness and irreligion of his victims' language. But the proper defense (if a modern critic wants one)[40] is—as Congreve also says—that one cannot represent vicious and foolish characters without making them speak viciously and foolishly. This principle goes back to Aristotle and was expounded by Dennis.[41] Nevertheless, the question how far Congreve's works sanction the amorality they display remains an issue for his admirers.[42]

38. *Preface to the Fables*, last paragraph, in *Essays*, II, 272.
39. *Amendments of Mr. Collier's False and Imperfect Citations*, in *Complete Works*, ed. Montagu Summers (London: Nonesuch Press, 1923), III, 172.
40. Cf. L. C. Knights, "Restoration Comedy: The Reality and the Myth," *Explorations* (London: Chatto and Windus, 1946), pp. 131-49.
41. *A Defence of Sir Fopling Flutter*, in *Critical Works*, II, 241-50.
42. Cf. Aubrey Williams, "Poetical Justice, the Contrivances of Providence, and the Works of William Congreve," *ELH* 35 (1968): 540–

I have illustrated the gap between theory and practice so profusely because it demonstrates the deep awareness these writers had of their methods of implication. A reader not familiar with their deviousness might underestimate their subtlety. I hope my range of examples will sharpen such a reader's expectations.

Besides, even a careful scholar sometimes leans too heavily on the generalizations which eighteenth-century authors give us concerning their aims and techniques.[43] In my view they are often least direct when they sound direct, and most artful when they sound artless. In the studies that follow, I generally trust the poet's text rather than his commentary on it; and I try to show that the four talents examined here deserve the closest attention to their secondary meanings.

65; and Maximillian Novak, *William Congreve* (New York: Twayne, 1971), pp. 58–71. Professor Williams carries his argument further in *An Approach to Congreve* (New Haven: Yale University Press, 1979).

43. P. K. Elkin, in his chapter on "Personal Reference" (*The Augustan Defence of Satire*, pp. 118–45), seems to me over-ready to take literally the assurances of Dryden, Swift, and Pope.

CHAPTER I

Dryden the Playwright

In his serious plays Dryden employs theatrical designs, or a dramaturgy, that audiences of our own time may connect not with tragedy but with comedy. A single example will make clear what I mean. This is an episode from one of the most fascinating plays of the seventeenth century, *The Conquest of Granada.*

Dryden called *The Conquest of Granada* a tragedy, and wrote it in two parts, each of five acts. The events take place during the year 1492, when the armies of Ferdinand and Isabella are closing in on the last stronghold of the Moors in Granada. As Dryden tells the story, one of the Moorish ladies, named Lyndaraxa, has a monstrous ambition to be a queen. She also happens to be dazzlingly beautiful, irresistibly seductive, and diabolically treacherous. Lyndaraxa will marry anybody who can place her on a throne.

Regrettably, the king of Granada, Boabdelin, is already equipped with a bride; so Lyndaraxa cannot go straight to the top. But Boabdelin has a younger brother, Abdalla, who is ambitious and susceptible. Lyndaraxa therefore encourages Abdalla to overthrow Boabdelin. With the help of the lady's fellow tribesmen, Abdalla does dislodge the king, who takes refuge in the Alhambra.

Abdalla, intoxicated by his victory, gives us a lesson in the misplacement of confidence by establishing his beloved Lyndaraxa as governess of the citadel of the Albazyn. He himself leaves her there and proceeds to rejoin his embattled followers, planning now to kill his brother, the dethroned Boabdelin.

At this point, the real hero of the play, a Herculean young conqueror named Almanzor, chooses to shift sides; and so he comes to the aid of Boabdelin. Led by Almanzor, the royal forces now beat back those of the usurper; and Abdalla, after his moment in purple, flees alone to find safety in the fortress of the Albazyn. He innocently supposes that Lyndaraxa will do all she can to rescue and comfort the man who has sacrificed his honor in order to set a crown on her head.

As Abdalla approaches the Albazyn, he hails a sentry who then challenges him; and the following exchanges take place:

Soldier: What orders for admittance do you bring?
Abdalla: Slave, my own orders: look, and know the king.
Soldier: I know you; but my charge is so severe,
  That none, without exception, enter here.
Abdalla: Traitor, and rebel! thou shalt shortly see
  Thy orders are not to extend to me.
Lyndaraxa [*above*]: What saucy slave so rudely does exclaim,
  And brands my subject with a rebel's name?
Abdalla: Dear Lyndaraxa, haste; the foes pursue.
Lyndaraxa: My lord, the Prince Abdalla, is it you?
  I scarcely can believe the words I hear;
  Could you so coarsely treat my officer?
Abdalla: He forced me; but the danger nearer draws:
  When I am entered, you shall know the cause.
Lyndaraxa: Entered! Why, have you any business here?
Abdalla: I am pursued, the enemy is near.
Lyndaraxa: Are you pursued, and do you thus delay
  To save yourself? Make haste, my lord, away.
Abdalla: Give me not cause to think you mock my grief:
  What place have I, but this, for my relief?
Lyndaraxa: This favour does your handmaid much oblige,

But we are not provided for a siege:
My subjects few; and their provision thin;
The foe is strong without, we weak within.
This to my noble lord may seem unkind,
But he will weigh it in his princely mind;
And pardon her, who does assurance want
So much, she blushes when she cannot grant.
Abdalla: Yes, you may blush; and you have cause to weep.
Is this the faith you promised me to keep?
Ah yet, if to a lover you will bring
No succour, give your succour to a king.
Lyndaraxa: A king is he, whom nothing can withstand;
Who men and money can with ease command.
A king is he, whom fortune still does bless;
He is a king, who does a crown possess.
If you would have me think that you are he,
Produce to view your marks of sovereignty;
But if yourself alone for proof you bring,
You're but a single person, not a king.
Abdalla: Ungrateful maid, did I for this rebel?
I say no more; but I have loved too well.
Lyndaraxa: Who but yourself did that rebellion move?
Did I e'er promise to receive your love?
Is it my fault you are not fortunate?
I love a king, but a poor rebel hate.
Abdalla: Who follow fortune, still are in the right;
But let me be protected here this night.
Lyndaraxa: The place to-morrow will be circled round;
And then no way will for your flight be found.
Abdalla: I hear my enemies just coming on;
                    [*Trampling within.*]
Protect me but one hour till they are gone.
Lyndaraxa: They'll know you have been here; it cannot be,
That very hour you stay, will ruin me:
For if the foe behold our interview,
I shall be thought a rebel too, like you.
Haste hence; and that your flight may prosperous prove,
I'll recommend you to the powers above.
                    (1 *The Conquest of Granada* V, i, 9–66)

To the action I have just outlined and the dialogue I have
quoted, the response of a modern reader is incredulity. Things

do not happen like that, and Dryden makes small effort to persuade us that they do. Lyndaraxa's strength as a *femme fatale* is given, not documented. Abdalla's ambition may be acceptable, because we bring to the theater a belief that men naturally desire all the power they can get. But we do not nowadays believe that intense ambition is easily distracted by lust, or that an unconquerable warrior will change sides so impulsively as Almanzor does.

The suddenness of the turnabouts produces another unfortunate response in a modern reader. The action does not seem tragic or pathetic, or even serious. Our anxiety is hardly aroused on behalf of figures who expose themselves so often and unexpectedly to strenuous moral conflicts, especially when their moral ideals touch few chords in our modern sensibilities. The design of the drama might seem closer to comedy than to tragedy.

What is the charm that rescues Dryden's serious plays from these dangers? It is the use the poet makes of his opportunities. When Lyndaraxa gives her definition of a king—"he, whom fortune still [i.e., always] does bless," etc.—the toughness with which her aphoristic couplets defy moral principle resolves any doubt as to the ultimate implications of the episode. The lines reverberate with memories of 1649 and 1660. They challenge the listener to choose between law and force.

On Abdalla's side, the element of surprise gains interest from the workings of distributive justice. Whether we care for him or not, we must enjoy the sense that he deserves his ordeal not only for his treachery but for his gullibility as well.

There is another attraction more pervasive than the balance of cheat against cheat. This is the general level of Dryden's style. The refinement of Lyndaraxa's language makes a delicious contrast to the ugly audacity of her motives. Whether or not the scene be classified as serious, the attentive listener must enjoy the irony of sentences like,

> This to my noble lord may seem unkind,
> But he will weigh it in his princely mind.

Such pleasures exist through the whole range of Dryden's serious plays, and they depend on his dramaturgy. Listeners who delight in them will tolerate the improbabilities in return for such benefits.

Other aspects of Dryden's genius appear in the scene I have quoted at such length. It may bring smiles to many lips, but it has a larger significance than a quick reader might suppose. One must enjoy the extraordinary modulations of emotion (which Dryden always prided himself on exhibiting). One must observe the continual shifts in Abdalla's tone, the steady revelation of Lyndaraxa's egoism. One must respond to the almost stichomythic debate—a standard feature of Dryden's dramaturgy— that marks the path to a reversal of our expectations. One must admire the ingenuity of Lyndaraxa's reasons, for Dryden prided himself on his powers of argument. "The favourite exercise of his mind was ratiocination," said Johnson.[1]

Contrary to what the ironies might suggest, Lyndaraxa will at last enjoy her own split second as a queen and will then suffer a dignified and moving death near the end of the second part of *The Conquest of Granada*. During the scene before us, her fate is visibly presaged. For she stands unmoving as she looks down securely from a wall of the Albazyn, and an isolated Abdalla paces the ground on foot as he humbly pleads below. Their relative levels and movements imply the relation of her power to his impotence; but they also foreshadow ironically her ultimate catastrophe as she falls from a brief height.

In this scene one must also come to understand that the dialogue implies serious political doctrine. The weakling Abdalla and the villainous Lyndaraxa misguidedly agree that kingship means power without responsibility, that fortune rather than providence raises men to royalty, that if rebellion succeeds, it legitimizes a usurper. In the course of the play, all these principles will be roundly contradicted; and when Granada falls to King Ferdinand, the reason will be not merely his military re-

1. "Life of Dryden," *Lives of the Poets*, ed. G. B. Hill (Oxford: Clarendon Press, 1905), I, 459.

sources but also his legal right and divine sanction. Once more the echoes of 1649 and 1660 will be audible.

The scene therefore illustrates several features that I wish to examine further: Dryden's willingness to suspend probability and simplify character; his apparent wavering between comic and tragic modes; his fascination with modulations of tone; his employment of the play (from time to time) as a vehicle for political theory; his readiness to use spectacle to imply meaning, but his preference for rhetoric and poetic. The scene only touches on his theory of sexual passion and very faintly alludes to his view of religion—two other themes I shall deal with.

Before proceeding, I must comment on the genre of Dryden's serious plays. It would be an error to associate his use of the term "tragedy" with works like *Oedipus Rex*, *Phèdre*, or *Othello*. Shakespeare's *Cymbeline* and perhaps *Coriolanus* would come closer to Dryden's idea. Certainly, any number of plays by Beaumont and Fletcher would. For Dryden's methods of implying meanings in drama spring from an eagerness to produce certain effects—effects appropriate to romance.

Wonder was an emotion he enjoyed nourishing. In his plots he looked for opportunities to start one action after another with surprising yet continuous changes of direction. So he designed his plays around sudden reversals of behavior, transformations of emotion, ambivalent alternations of intention. Dryden delighted in ratiocinative debate and rhetorical display. Although his lines of action would not bear very complicated characters, he could infuse life into his people through the energy of their disputation, intellectual duels forcing the emotional permutations. One reason he favored double plots was that the movements of one set of characters could echo, undercut, or invert the implications of another.

So also to make quick changes of action and intention possible, Dryden devised plots that engaged polarities within polarities: one pair of lovers at cross purposes with another pair, all of them troubled by fathers who frown on their daughters' choices, and in addition with the suitors of both ladies caught up in tribal or partisan quarrels dividing a nation which is itself at war against an invader who lays claim to the throne. In the development of such a play, all the lovers can enjoy peripety upon peripety as the young men gain or lose battles or mistresses, arguments or thrones, honor or parental approval. The aim Dryden set himself was not to make such turns intrinsically probable, or expressive of inner character; rather, it was to expound the various oppositions in language so seductive that the issue of probability would seem irrelevant.[2]

Sexual passion is central to Dryden's scheme. In *The Conquest of Granada*, no sooner does King Boabdelin feel secure on his throne than he abandons himself to jealousy of the superlatively heroic Almanzor, because he quite correctly fears that Queen Almahide loves that mirror of knighthood. Yet as soon as an enemy threatens Boabdelin's rule, Almahide invokes Almanzor's bottomless devotion to herself, and spurs him yet once more into rescuing the loathed rival. To such oscillations only a certain concept of sexual passion is appropriate, and we shall shortly examine it.

But first I should like to point out the connection between the pleasure of debate and the pleasure found in surprising reversals. As the disputes of Dryden's characters proceed, their key terms tend to alter—indignation collapsing into remorse, loyalty changing to rebellion, love into hatred or jealousy. The course of the debate leads to a revelation of fresh facts about one of the antagonists, or to a recognition of his inner nature; and this then creates the longed-for peripety.

In *The Conquest of Granada* an admirable warrior named Ozmyn is hated by the father of the woman he adores; but he nobly defends that bitter old man, Selin, from the rage of his own father when all three meet during a battle. The audience has the pleasure of hearing a furious debate between Ozmyn and Abenamar, his own father, over the fate of Selin. In a rage, Abenamar leads his soldiers against both his son and old Selin, but only after a stichomythic exchange. When help arrives to

2. Cf. the discussion by Moody Prior in *The Language of Tragedy* (New York: Columbia University Press, 1947), pp. 156–58.

repulse Abenamar, he renews the debate with a magnificently snarling climax:

> By no entreaties, by no length of time,
> Will I be won; but, with my latest breath,
> I'll curse thee here, and haunt thee after death,
>
> (2 *The Conquest of Granada* II, i, 69–71)

Abenamar must now withdraw, leaving Ozmyn with his beloved Benzayda and her father Selin. Yet all the vocalizing is not wasted. The external force of combat, and the internal pressure of emotion given voice, work together on Selin with the force of revelation. He acknowledges at last the nobility of his daughter's admirer and is tearfully reconciled to Ozmyn. Here is a pattern that affords ample and fascinating scope for Dryden's talents, as emotions rise, sharpen, and transform themselves in furious repartee which then slides into elegantly pathetic self-analysis and moral conversion. We may now proceed to observe the pattern in Dryden's handling of sexuality, and thereby to understand why elementary carnal passion has so much work to do in Dryden's plays.

The turns and counterturns of Dryden's plots get their changing directions from the wills of the individual characters. These wills, however, must not be predictable, because Dryden's rhetoric and drama depend on surprise. Love therefore is brought to operate inside a personality as an energy matching the weight of domestic duties, tribal alliances, civil war, and foreign invasion outside the person. Public loyalties and betrayals collide with private lust and jealousy. Other passions—avarice, revenge, the thirst for power—are more steady and less capricious than the spasms of sex; they are weaker servants of Dryden's genius.

In *Tyrannick Love* a conjurer named Nigrinus is asked to foretell the outcome of the emperor's passion for the Princess Catherine of Alexandria. Nigrinus replies,

> Of Wars, and Bloodshed, and of dire Events,
> Of Fates, and fighting Kings, their Instruments,
> I could with greater certainty foretell;

Love only does in doubts and darkness dwell.
For, like a wind, it in no quarter stays;
But points and veers each hour a thousand ways.
On Women Love depends, and they on Will;
Chance turns their Orb while Destiny sits still.

(IV, 3–10)

Love determines action; and love must be sudden and un-controllable, easily converted to jealousy or hate. If sexual passion were of slow growth, consistent, or predictable, it would undermine precisely those features of a play that fire Dryden's imagination. As an abrupt, totally engulfing flood, love and its mutations lend themselves to his genius; and in the undulations of these feelings Dryden displays the splendid resourcefulness of his language.

To allow the waves of feeling to move as far as possible, love must sink quickly into related passions. Jealousy and hatred are its undersides. When frustrated, the furious desire to love becomes a rage to kill. So in *Tyrannick Love*, Maximin's ardor for Catherine reacts from her disdain, to deliver her up to hideous tortures. Dryden is almost obsessional in his identification of love with death. This is not merely a metaphor or double entendre. At the point of its gratification sexual excitement dissolves the self as death does. The two experiences—death and sexual ecstasy—are alternative forms of the same loss of identity.

An example of what I mean appears in *The Indian Emperour*. The setting is Mexico during the Spanish invasion. The Emperor Montezuma has captured the virtuous Spanish general Cortez and imprisoned him in chains. An Indian princess Almeria, whom the emperor adores, wishes to avenge her dead brother and to save her country by murdering Cortez. Almeria gains access to the prison and finds Cortez asleep. Drawing a dagger, she wakes him up so he may suffer the terror of watching death approach. To her astonishment, he meets her threat without flinching.

The audience sees Almeria upright, dagger raised; Cortez beneath, loaded with chains. Precisely at this moment, with no warning of any sort, she falls in love with him. After quarreling with herself, she tries again to stab Cortez, but only lowers her dagger. The phallic symbolism of the weapon rising and falling suggests her emotional distraction. Love has smothered the wish for revenge; and Almeria abandons the plan of killing her nation's enemy.

What Dryden gains by this turn is the gorgeous opportunity to exhibit a frantic princess, exotically costumed, debating mind against heart over her sudden transformation, and then gradually, indirectly, revealing to the astonished Cortez, in spite of her shame, the cause of her passivity. As she does so, he responds with a matching inner conflict. A new *frisson* disturbs the love Cortez already has felt for Montezuma's daughter Cydaria. The struggle within Almeria's breast starts one within his own. After she leaves, the tormented Cortez thinks of Cydaria and ends the scene with a string of lapidary paradoxes:

> In wishing nothing we enjoy still most;
> For ev'n our wish is in possession lost:
> Restless we wander to a new desire,
> And burn our selves by blowing up the fire:
> We toss and turn about our feav'rish will,
> When all our ease must come by lying still:
> For all the happiness mankind can gain
> Is not in pleasure, but in rest from pain.
>
> (IV, i, 107–14)

As an example of how sexual passion provides the fuel for Dryden's emotional fireworks and his marvelous reversals of direction, even the episode of Cortez and Almeria seems low-keyed when it is compared with another, in Dryden's superb play *Aureng-Zebe*. This time the setting is India, at the court of the Great Mogul in Agra, during the year 1660. The old emperor has, by his deceased first wife, a wholly admirable heir, Aureng-Zebe—brave, loyal, obedient. But his lusty second wife, Nourmahal, wishes her own son to succeed to the throne. Nourmahal is much younger than the septuagenarian emperor and finds him a contemptibly flaccid lover. In a sudden turn of the plot, her son Morat does win the emperor's approval, and Aureng-Zebe finds himself condemned to die. Nourmahal requests the privilege of poisoning him; the emperor consents; and the blameless hero is released in her recognizance.

Nourmahal is now left on stage with her favorite slave, to enjoy the prospect of indulging a merciless disposition. But she stuns the confidant—and the audience—by announcing that she loves Aureng-Zebe and expects to seduce him. In Act IV we discover the blameless victim awaiting his ambiguous doom in Nourmahal's chambers. When the empress enters, she of course procrastinates; and a long dialogue ensues in which Aureng-Zebe urges her to speed the execution while she wants him to feel grateful for the delay—which incidentally tickles the prurience of the listeners. It is characteristic of Dryden that sexual themes should inspire him with suggestive imagery and with plays on words. Nor is he above toying with the antique pun on "die." Nourmahal herself has made much of that handy device in the talk with her slave. During the debate with Aureng-Zebe, the association of love with death grows more and more ambiguously titillating. At one point the hero says,

> I need not haste the end of Life to meet;
> The precipice is just beneath my feet.

Nourmahal replies,

> Think not my sense of Virtue is no small:
> I'll rather leap down first, and break your fall.
> (V, 51–54)

The audience of course is aware of the insinuation, but Aureng-Zebe is deliciously unresponsive. As he ignores his stepmother's heavy language, she must come closer and closer to declaring her incestuous lust until at last she fulsomely reports an aphrodisiac dream in which the goddess Venus reproached Aureng-Zebe for disregarding her caresses. Properly horrified, even the guileless hero now understands that he is to play Hippolytus to his stepmother's Phaedra. Though he tries to repel her intentions, Nourmahal has slipped beyond self-restraint, and persists in her blandishments until Dryden can finally offer us a gorgeous peripety, in which the love-death motif makes an

unpredictable double somersault. Revolted by Nourmahal's infatuation, Aureng-Zebe tells her of his loathing. At once, she
holds out a dagger and asks him to kill her. He refuses. At once
she produces a cup of poison and asks him to drink it. One feels
that an elemental rage is continuously at work, only shifting, as
it is frustrated, from one outlet to another. The fury of love
easily becomes the fury of suicide or murder; the phallic dagger
gives way to the vaginal cup:

> *Aureng-Zebe*: In me a horrour of my self you raise;
> Curs'd by your love, and blasted by your praise.
> You find new ways to prosecute my Fate;
> And your least guilty passion was your Hate.
> *Nourmahal*: I beg my death, if you can Love deny,
> [*Offering him a dagger.*]
> *Aureng-Zebe*: I'll grant you nothing; no, not ev'n to die.
> *Nourmahal*: Know then, you are not half so kind as I.
> [*Stamps with her foot.*]
> [*Enter mutes, some with swords drawn, one with a cup.*]
> You've chosen, and may now repent too late.
> Behold th'effect of what you wish'd, my hate.
> This cup, a cure for both our ills has brought:
> You need not fear a philtre in the draught.
> [*Taking the cup to present him.*]
> *Aureng-Zebe*: All must be poison which can come from thee;
> But this the least.
> [*Receiving it from her.*]
> (IV, 153–65)

Of course, Aureng-Zebe is saved as he lifts the poison to his lips.
Thus we see once more how Dryden works out his pattern
of debate, emotional climax, and peripety. We see how useful
the capricious impulse of sexuality is for his purposes; and we
hear how adequate his language is to the occasion. Another element is wanted to heighten the excitement. This is a hero whose
response to love should be marvelous. It must not be one who
gives himself normally to affairs of the heart. Tenderness should
be the last attribute we expect of him. He must be not a Troilus
but a Hotspur. His attachment must be to glory, not voluptuous-
ness. In *Tyrannick Love*, when the elderly emperor Maximin

finds himself unable to withstand the beauty of the princess Catherine, he says,

> This love that never could my youth engage,
> Peeps out his coward head to dare my age.
>
> (III, 1–2)

So Dryden's heroes are larger than life. Their physical courage is unblemished. Their spirit is magnanimous. In fact, even a villain if he is grand enough, can stir us with his greatness of heart.[3] Such uncompromising, sublime natures devote themselves to duty, honor, reputation. When Almanzor, in *The Conquest of Granada*, looks on the face of Almahide, when he drops the tone of Achilles and talks like Orlando sickening for Angelica, our pleasure in his rhapsody depends on our regarding him as a fire-tempered warrior who lives without sensual indulgence. His submission to love is all the more wonderful and sudden:

> Arms, and the dusty field I less admire,
> And soften strangely in some new desire;
> Honour burns in me not so fiercely bright,
> But pales as fires when mastered by the light:
> E'en while I speak and look, I change yet more,
> And now am nothing that I was before.
> I'm numbed, and fixed, and scarce my eyeballs move;
> I fear it is the lethargy of love!
> 'Tis he; I feel him now in ev'ry part:
> Like a new lord he vaunts about my heart;
> Surveys, in state, each corner of my breast,
> While poor fierce I, that was, am dispossessed.
>
> (part 1, V, 323–34)

When I speak of the "adequacy" of the language to the occasion, I do not pretend that it peculiarly reveals a unique personality, or that it is close to the speech we might use in actually suffering the emotion. I mean that Dryden finds images

---

3. Corneille says of his utterly evil Cléopatre, "[Tous] ses crimes sont accompagnés d'une grandeur d'ame qui a quelque chose de si haut, qu'en meme temps qu'on déteste ses actions, on admire la source dont elles partent" (preface to *Rodogune*, quoted in Dryden, *Works*, X, 392). There is a sublimity of villainy as well as of heroism; and I suppose Dryden intended Nourmahal, as well as Maximin, to exemplify such a character.

and turns of phrase elegantly appropriate to the theme and the moment. When Almanzor wishes to kill himself, Almahide forbids him; and he replies,

> What cause can I for living longer, give,
> But a dull lazy habitude to live?

She urges him to treat his love for her as a brief infatuation, and to let it pass naturally:

> 'Twas but a dream; where truth had not a place:
> A scene of fancy, mov'd so swift a pace
> And shifted, that you can but think it was:
> Let, then, the short vexatious vision pass.

> (part 1, V, i, 414–15, 428–31)

Expressions like "dull lazy habitude to live" and "short vexatious vision" are fresh, memorable, and frequent in Dryden's plays. Readers with an ear for dramatic verse will cherish them.

If we now look back at the large design I have been sketching, we may see the issue of genre in a stronger light; for I think Dryden's design implies an attitude toward social institutions and moral traditions that belongs to a particular literary form. It is a commonplace of scholarship that Dryden thought of tragedy in terms of epic. He labeled *The Conquest of Granada* a tragedy; but in the dedication he described it as "heroic poetry" and mentioned only epics among his models. This terminology can help us if we agree on the meaning of "epic" for Dryden. The trouble is that he was much influenced by a kind of epic that lacks the dignity we associate with the genre. The *Iliad* and the *Aeneid* are the first examples of epic that come to the modern mind. If we think of later works, *Paradise Lost* is what we know best. Dryden accepted these models. But he also said that he took his definition of a heroic play from Ariosto's *Orlando Furioso* ("Of Heroique Plays," para. 3). Now Ariosto's masterpiece is remote indeed from anything we might call tragedy. It is self-conscious, ironic, heroic, and pathetic by turns. Brave knights turn aside from glorious missions in order to pursue ravishing beauties. An imperial princess falls in love with a humble page and carries him off to be her prince. One

plot casually interrupts another; the interrupted stories are unexpectedly renewed and continued. Low moods break in on
high moods; magical and supernatural events of the greatest
elaboration displace probable chains of action. The heroes of
Orlando Furioso are more than human but are also subject to
extraordinary whims, impulses, and changes of heart.

It is this tradition of ironic romance in which Dryden's most
serious drama participates: a tradition of courtly, mannered acting out of chivalric ideals illuminated by Renaissance scepticism. It implies a nostalgia for the pure heroism of romance,
along with a regretful criticism of it. Dryden and his audience
recalled the uncompromising idealism that dragged England
into civil war. They longed to recapture such sublimity in their
imagination. They wished the royal court to color their lives
with it. But they realized it would also be inappropriate to the
stability of government and society on which the comfort of
their lives depended. The mixture of warm admiration and ironic
detachment explains Dryden's treatment of his superhuman
characters.

We shall come back to Dryden's conception of a hero. But
I have completed my sketch of his dramaturgy and will go on
with his methods of implication. In trying to decide whether the
doctrines expressed in a play are those of Dryden or of his characters, one meets tantalizing difficulties. First, Dryden produces
his allusions or doctrines spasmodically. Every now and then he
breaks into a passage of political implication, then returns simply
to the action of his play. What is worse, he sometimes gives his
own doctrines to evil characters. For one cannot be sure, simply
because a character is reprehensible, that he always quarrels with
the playwright. Besides, Dryden simply enjoyed arguing on both
sides of a question. He prided himself on his ability to defend a
point of view which in fact he disagreed with. As a result, one
hears characters speaking very persuasively indeed for doctrines
which the play invites us to resist.

A good example of the problem is a discussion of religious
zeal in *Tyrannick Love*. The wicked, pagan emperor and his

officer Placidius condemn Christianity in language that certainly refers to Puritanism:

> The silly crowd, by factious teachers brought
> To think that faith untrue their youth was taught,
> Run on in new opinions blindly bold;
> Neglect, contemn, and then assault the old.
>
> (II, i, 143–56)

We could learn from passages in other works by Dryden that he wholly agreed with the sentiments of the monster, that he expected the audience to apply them not to the persecuted early Christians but to the Calvinist rebels of the 1640s. If we did not know the play was written to honor Queen Catherine, consort of Charles II, and that it was produced for spectators sympathetic with the court, the passage could become a crux of interpretation. But the nature of the audience and the attitude of the playwright are not in doubt, and neither is the implication of the speeches. In other words, the explication of the meaning depends not on rhetorical analysis but on the establishment of allusions to external reality—on context.

For purposes of implication, the obvious advantage of the drama is the use of spectacle to enrich meaning. One finds telling examples of this in Dryden's plays, especially when he deals with political or religious themes. Baroque stagecraft favored symbolic and sensational productions, which throve under royal patronage, as monarchs aspiring to absolutism imitated the visual and musical devices of the Counter-Reformation in order to strengthen their own association with divinity.

So it is natural that marvelous spectacular effects should have been among the strong appeals of *Tyrannick Love*. The story is that of St. Catherine of Alexandria defying the Roman emperor Maximin and converting his courtiers to Christianity. Dryden took advice from King Charles II when he wrote the play, and he intended the work as a compliment to Queen Catherine. Her majesty had been painted as St. Catherine five years before the play was produced; and the artist was the Belgian Huysmans, whose style has been described as "more nearly allied to the Continental Catholic Baroque than Lely's Protestant idiom."[4] Besides having spirits and an angel descending from above, and St. Catherine in her bed rising from below, the play offers a large scene of an elysium, commissioned at great expense from the painter Isaac Fuller.[5] The alliance of God, king, and playwright is remarkable.

In general, the very paraphernalia of royalty and court ceremony can dignify the idea of monarchy, a principle which belongs to the substance of tragedy and of history plays. It was natural for Dryden to find opportunities for implication through spectacle when he touched on political motifs; and he turned such opportunities to ingenious profit at the end of *All for Love*, when Serapion enters to see the bodies of Antony and Cleopatra enthroned, upright, in full regalia; for here we meet a visible sign that the empire of passion is more exalted than the empire of the world. In such spectacle, the judgment implied by the whole play is clarified and embodied.

An earlier stage of the quarrel between political responsibility and sensual indulgence is more subtly visible in Act III of *All for Love*. Here a train of pathetic appeals has been inching Antony away from sexual passion and toward statesmanship. A long-awaited peripety occurs as he turns back from an emotional debate with his wife Octavia to his other side, where an old, dear friend, Dolabella, stands. When Dolabella supports Octavia's call to duty, Antony turns again and finds his beloved officer Ventidius pleading with him. Octavia now produces Antony's two children and comes up before him with them: one little girl holds his arms; the other hugs his waist, making a vertical, triangular composition. Standing in the center of the larger triangle of his friends and his wife, and with the two little girls up against him, Antony looks at Ventidius, who cries, "Emperor"; next he looks at Dolabella, who cries, "Friend"; then at Octavia, who cries, "Husband," and finally at the children, who cry, "Father." The modulation is from the most

4. Ellis Waterhouse, *Painting in Britain, 1530 to 1790* (London: Penguin Books, 1953), p. 65, cited in Dryden, *Works*, X, 382.
5. Dryden, *Works*, X, 380–81.

public and dignified to the most private and pathetic obligations, with the emotional pressure symbolized by the two triangles, one within the other. When Antony yields to domestic morality, the geometrical figures dissolve.

Jean Hagstrum has suggested that the very balance of the debates (Cleopatra against Ventidius) and the symmetry of the groupings on Dryden's stage might suggest a traditional emblem of moral dilemmas, the Renaissance topos of the Choice of Hercules.[6] But of course, older traditions going back to the morality play would encourage the use of a visible contrast between right and wrong.

Normally, even in drama, Dryden relies on language to convey his meaning, whether explicit or implicit. His use of spectacle implies little, except as enhancement of the speeches. This principle certainly applies to *Tyrannick Love*, for all its stage effects. It is in a public debate that Catherine demonstrates the superiority of Christianity to paganism. Yet religion does offer opportunities that politics cannot surpass. Vestments and ceremonies produce their effect in the theater as in the church, although Dryden took little advantage of such opportunities. Once in a while, he adds ironies to a scene with ecclesiastical properties. In *An Evening's Love* two young Englishmen irreverently flirt with Spanish girls in a chapel. In *The Spanish Friar* and *The Assignation* religion and vice are paired in a time-honored, overripe lubricity. But there are more interesting examples. I shall give one from *The Indian Emperour*.

Here, in Act V, a remarkable discussion of natural religion takes place. In the middle of the stage are Montezuma, the captured emperor of Mexico, and his high priest, both of them stretched on racks, with a torturer apiece ready to tighten the cords that pull their bones out of the joints. On one side, a Spanish priest confronts the Mexican priest; on the other side, the greedy conquistador Pizarro confronts Montezuma.

In order to make the emperor tell where his gold is hidden, the Spaniards order the torturers to rack the prisoners. The

6. Jean H. Hagstrum, *The Sister Arts* (Chicago: University of Chicago Press, 1958), pp. 190–97.

Christian priest urges them to tighten the cords and warns Montezuma that he will suffer even worse pains in hell. A debate now follows between the native priest and the European, as to the merits of Roman Catholicism and the Mexicans' faith. It is the layman Montezuma who intervenes between the quarreling clerics to recommend a natural religion more universal, rational, and reliable than that of Christian revelation.

The visible scene clearly favors the central, martyred Mexicans and depreciates the flanking Europeans. With his uncorrupted, primitive reason, Montezuma also rises above the limitations of both churchmen. At the same time, he shows more courage and endurance than his own high priest, who dies under torture after behaving himself ignominiously. When the magnanimous Cortez enters, he at once puts an end to the torture and releases Montezuma. But the broken emperor cannot walk. As Cortez helps him down, he embraces Montezuma and cries out,

> Ah! Father! Father! what do I endure
> To see these wounds my pity cannot cure.
> (V, ii, 117–18)

The parallel with Christ is inescapable; the spectacle must remind the audience of the descent from the cross; and the implication is obvious: that virtuous laymen and uncorrupted reason are closer to true Christianity than the greed, ambition, and hypocrisy of priests.

A far subtler handling of spectacle occurs in the last act of *Don Sebastian*, when Alvarez tries to caution the hero and heroine against the danger of incest. After a series of speeches dealing with the marriages of their parents, he has Dorax produce a document in which the father of Sebastian confesses his involvement with the mother of Almeyda. When even this evidence is scorned and destroyed by the furious girl, Alvarez falls back on the rings that each of the young couple wears. As he stands priestlike before the pair, takes the rings, and puts them together, the old man enacts a reversal of the wedding ritual. In dumb show he anticipates the revelation that the sacrament of matrimony has been violated, and he foreshadows the denouement of the play.

If we now go on from religion to politics, we are again reminded what a delicate matter it is to know whether or not a dramatic character is conveying the playwright's doctrine. When we are blessed, the author grants us some signal that we are to expect political allusions. Once we are alerted and look for parallels between the drama and public events, such parallels will commonly appear as material not perfectly assimilated—sentiments not necessary to the characterizations or the action. They should of course reinforce one another; the same point of view should emerge from the various allusions. Yet this seldom means that the allusions will be continuous, or that we may interpret any long section of the play systematically as implying doctrine. Like allegory, political allusion is discontinuous, bowing to the strength of the narrative line. Normally, one has no warning of the correspondences that leap out.

I can illustrate my meaning with an excellent play that Dryden wrote when he was almost sixty years old. The poet could no longer speak out loud and clear on politics. His patron, the Roman Catholic James II had fled, now lived in exile, and was fighting vainly to win back his throne. The new king was James's own son-in-law, the Dutch Calvinist William III, who had replaced Dryden as poet laureate by Shadwell, his ancient enemy. Dryden, now a Roman Catholic himself, with little money and no power, could not openly argue in support of James. But he could sneer at those who had deserted his royal master after accepting royal favors. He could also sneer at those who followed the new king for the sake of the riches and titles he might heap on them.

Dryden opens his play *Amphitryon* with a prologue bemoaning recent efforts to weaken political satire; and he refers in it to another prologue of his, so provocative that the government suppressed it. This signal he immediately amplifies with the first 150 lines of his play, in which Jupiter is described as an earthly king, the family of gods sounds like a royal court, and the relations between Jupiter and the inferior gods are expressed as those between a king and his subjects. These analogies have nothing to do with the main action of the play; and yet the references to the English government are sometimes dagger-edged.

After this section, the listener must be hard of hearing to miss the parallels. Jupiter and Mercury become, at moments, spokesmen for the English court and the parliamentary opposition just after the Glorious Revolution. As an instance of how far Dryden could go, I shall only mention a passage openly comparing Apollo to the English landed gentry, who disapprove of the government but lack the persistence and energy wanted to carry through their policies.

> But you Brother Phoebus, are but a meer Country Gentleman, that never comes to Court; that are abroad all day on Horseback, making Visits about the World; are drinking all Night, and in your Cups are still rayling at the Government: O these Patriots, these bumpkin Patriots, are a very silly sort of Animal.
>
> (I, i, 133–43)

In general, the allusions are censorious, as a quiet political implication is likely to be; for one normally shouts compliments to those in power, but murmurs insults. Dryden's implications range over the usual complaints of the country party against the self-servers in Westminster: the tyranny, avarice, injustice, and irresponsibility of the king,[7] the frivolity and treachery of the courtiers,[8] the unsteadiness of the opposition,[9] the corruption of the judiciary,[10] the hypocrisy of priests,[11] and the uniform venality of mankind. It is not an idealized picture of the institutions of government.

The play went into production about a year and a half after the Glorious Revolution, and only a few months after the two kings—William III and James II—collided in Ireland at the head of their armies: both crowned heads were now asking their confused and bitterly divided people to acknowledge them.

7. I, i, 57–86, 116–18, 131–32; V, i, 64.
8. I, i, 147–49.   9. I, i, 138–43.
10. V, i, 13–16.   11. V, i, 130.

Keeping the chaotic situation in mind, I am tempted to brood over larger possibilities; and I shall just touch on these.

In the play, Amphitryon returns home from war to find another person occupying his own place. This is the king of the gods, Jupiter, who has decided to exercise Amphitryon's prerogatives in the bedchamber. Jupiter takes care, of course, to look exactly like the man whose place he is usurping. He also distributes money and gifts freely and wins over the servants of the family. Dryden draws an explicit parallel between women who sell their bodies and statesmen in power; the word "ends" in the passage is a pun:

> All seek their ends; and each wou'd other cheat.
> They onely seem to hate, and seem to love;
> But int'rest[12] is the point on which they move.
> Their friends are foes; and foes are friends agen;
> And, in their turns, are knaves, and honest men.
> Our iron age is grown an age of gold:
> 'Tis who bids most; for all men wou'd be sold.
>
> (IV, 551–57)

This speech is delivered by the presiding genius of the age—Mercury, god of thieves.

At the end, in a traditional use of spectacle, both the true Amphitryon and the false appear on the stage at once, with exactly the same appearance, and with both claiming to be head of the household. Hence my larger possibilities. It seems significant that the servants join the false Amphitryon, Jupiter, who has been so free with his bribes. The true Amphitryon has no claim on them except his virtues, his integrity and legitimacy. Is Dryden trying to account for the failure of the English people to rally behind his own patron (and their rightful king)?

In the splendidly comic scenes of the last act there are touches of pathos. When Charles II first came home from exile, Dryden celebrated his restoration in *Astraea Redux* by describing him as a bridegroom and England as a languishing bride. But here the true spouse is cast out, and his wife takes a

12. I.e., self-interest.

pretender into her bed. It is spectacle (a device appropriate to royalty) that brings out the implications; for we see the two Amphitryons juxtaposed, matching various sorts of evidence, and both of them refusing to yield. We also see it is the true Amphitryon who shows the heroic, impetuous character of figures like Almanzor; and alas we see it is the false Amphitryon who has the upper hand. Heroism is out of style along with integrity and legitimacy. A pharaoh reigns who knows not Joseph.

The nature of Dryden's interest in sexual passion did not make it easy for him to use spectacle as a means of implying his attitudes. But if voyeurism could not be fed with a twentieth-century diet, other proclivities could be. As love, hate, and jealousy clash—in Dryden's plays—with various kinds of obligation (revenge, patriotism, filial obedience), they suggest a division between pagan and Christian morality which at times can become explicit, as in *Tyrannick Love*, and lead us into religious themes. Dryden often deepens the idea of genital pleasure by the ancient bond between piety and sexual passion; for he evokes a doctrine of the sacredness of voluptuous indulgence. The joys of love become in his language not an embellishment of life but the focus of life.

In fact, Dryden's concept of sexual passion rarely escapes from the pagan mode. For him, what seems most fascinating in love is the change that comes over the mind when voluptuous desire takes possession of it—i.e., the undifferentiated carnal impulse. So consistent is Dryden's attitude that I think we may generalize it as implying a doctrine, and assert that for him the common denominator of all sexual relations was so great as to make ordinary distinctions seem trifling. When Almahide offers Almanzor sisterly tenderness in place of the physical ardor that drives him, he replies,

> A sisters love! that is so pall'd a thing!
> What pleasure can it to a lover bring?
> 'Tis like thin food to men in feavours spent;
> Just keeps alive; but gives no nourishment.
> (1 *The Conquest of Granada* V, i, 448–51)

Whether the emotion struck high personages or comic butts, worldly courtiers or pastoral innocents, whether it was natural or perverse, so long as it sprang from physical gratification—the delights of foreplay and orgasm—the appetite for that experience would constitute the defining principle of the relationship; and the relationship becomes, with military actions, one of the central metaphors of Dryden's poetry. War translates into love; love into war; monarch and nation are man and wife. So Mars and Venus blend and serve as the primary metaphors for religion and politics. "Amo; ergo sum," says Dryden.

Yet the theater of the 1690s was not so enlightened as to tolerate the visible enactment of sexual passion that we take for granted today. As if to compensate for the lack of voyeurist spectacle, Dryden elaborated the provocations of language. Restricted to these, he made his vocabulary crackle with ambiguity, innuendo, and double meaning. One is seldom mistaken when one imagines that the poet is being obscene. Never is his diction so evocative as when he treads the brink of pornography. Puns and metaphors start overtones until the listener feels divided between surprise at the poet's coarseness and fascination with his implications. When Lyndaraxa, as governess of the Albazyn, tries to seduce Almanzor, she offers him the citadel and her sexual parts in the same language, and even hints at being made pregnant by his "coming":

> Enter, brave sir; for, when you speak the word,
> These gates will open of their own accord.
> The genius of the place its lord will meet:
> And bend its tow'ry forehead to your feet.
> That little cittadel, which now you see,
> Shall then, the head of conquer'd nations be:
> And every turret, from your coming, rise
> The mother of some great metropolis.

When Almanzor refuses, because of his attachment to Almahide, he uses imagery suggesting castration, and Lyndaraxa responds with allusions to the darkness and closeness of the sexual act, adding a pun on "charity":

> *Almanzor*: My love's now grown so much a part of me,
> That life would, in the cure, endanger'd be.
> At least it like a limb cut off would show;
> And better dye than like a cripple goe.
> *Lyndaraxa*: You must be brought like mad men to their cure;
> And darkness first and next new bonds endure:
> Do you dark absence to your self ordain:
> And I, in charity, will find the chain.
>
> (2 *The Conquest of Granada* III, iii, 92–99, 136–43)

This figurative language is not tender or gentle but violent and swift, evoking sudden victories in war, or flooded rivers quickly overflowing. The poet plays constantly with the image of fire bursting out, dying down, smouldering, and flaring up. Such essential violence is the first principle of sexual passion and explains its relation to the destructiveness of jealousy and hate. The metaphors for love that Dryden affects often derive from field sports, warfare, tempests, conflagrations, and floods—phenomena that are themselves metaphors for one another. Such a tendency is convenient for an author whose plays abound in battles and whose soldiers use similes drawn from lovemaking to express their delight in war. Rarely does Dryden employ imagery to bring out the peculiar nature of the individual speaking. It is meaning that he illuminates, a concept of love that applies to heroes in general. The vehicles of his metaphors—flames, storms—rely on familiar emblems which an audience can identify and interpret without regard to the unique character.[13]

In many passages we may observe how the absence of visible gestures only brightens the implications of Dryden's words. So in *Tyrannick Love* the brutal emperor Maximin is audibly phallic in telling how he responds to the beauty of Catherine:

> My Love shoots up in tempests, as the Earth
> Is stirr'd and loosen'd in a blust'ring wind,
> Whose blasts to waiting flowers her womb unbind.
>
> (III, 6–8)

Again, in the First Part of *The Conquest of Granada*, when Almanzor stands in place and stares fixedly at Almahide, his

13. Cf. Prior, pp. 169–77.

imagery is both reductive and fast-moving; it puns on the language of sexual climax:

> Nay, I am Love; Love shot, and shot so fast,
> He shot himself into my breast at last.
>
> (III, 373-74)

The spasmodic repetitions of "love" and "shot," the lingering echoes of "fast" in "breast" and "last," suggest the moment of emission. So also in *Aureng-Zebe*, when the prince gives vent to his passion for Indamora, there is nothing soulful in the style:

> Oh, I could stifle you, with eager haste!
> Devour your kisses with my hungry taste! . . .
> Then hold you off and gaze! then, with new rage,
> Invade you, till my conscious limbs presage
> Torrents of joy, which all their banks o'erflow!
> So lost, so blest, as I but then could know!
>
> (IV, 535-42)

Once more, the imagery of invasion followed by that of fluid overflowing suggests ejaculation. In the whole passage of violent emotion, there is no word of tender sympathy with the beloved.

Dryden's ultimate reliance on language, rather than visible scene or gesture, gives him immense verve when his themes coincide—when sexuality, religion, and politics are blended in a climactic (if you will pardon the word) episode. The ending of *Don Sebastian* is such a moment. In this play the literary style abounds in eccentric images supporting eccentric themes. What dominates the language is a cluster of motifs inverting healthy human relationships.

The most interesting character, Dorax, sets the tone by speaking with a bitterness nourished by a distrust of all men. In an early scene an emblem of bestiality takes over the stage when Antonio, the main character of the secondary plot, must show himself off as an animal, compelled to go down on all fours and put himself through the paces of a horse. Perverse sexuality tinges the story. Dorax twice accuses other men of being homosexual. The hero and heroine commit incest.

Private and public treachery fill the action. Dorax himself, furious with the failure of his king, Don Sebastian, to reward his services, had deserted that admirable monarch, turned Mohammedan, and entered the service of the depraved Emperor of Barbary. A statesman and a priest poison Dorax independently but at the same time. The chief minister of the emperor persuades the latter's brother to overthrow him but only so the minister may then overthrow the brother. The Mufti, religious leader of the Moors, is a shameless hypocrite who uses religion as a screen for lust, avarice, and a thirst for power. (One thinks of the charges brought against Bishop Burnet by his enemies at the court of William III.) The motifs of salvation and damnation recur in the play but are turned about. Love and death are explicitly identified. The hero Sebastian is devoutly Catholic but loves a Moslem princess and almost commits the sin of suicide.

It is suggestive of Dryden's poetic instincts that he should not prepare for the denouement of his plot by a dramatic chain of probable motivations and causes—causes derived from essential character and leading one into the other—but rather by a cumulation of themes, images, and foreshadowings, by symmetries and reversals, that amass the figurative language to be employed in the final scenes. Almeyda is converted to Christianity in a mirror image of the renegadism of Dorax. She speaks of killing herself to avoid yielding to the emperor's passion, but Sebastian warns her that Christians may not commit suicide:

> Brutus and Cato might discharge their Souls,
> And give 'em Furlo's for another World:
> But we, like Centry's, are oblig'd to stand
> In starless Nights, and wait the 'pointed hour.
>   (II, i, 526–29)

She says her love for Sebastian is not carnal but sisterly:

> Mine is a flame so holy, and so clear,
> That the white taper leaves no soot behind;
> No smoak of Lust; but chast as Sisters love,

When coldly they return a Brothers kiss,
Without the zeal that meets at lovers mouths.
(II, i, 576–80)

Sebastian's speech anticipates his own furious attempt at suicide in the fifth act. The imagery of Almeyda's speech anticipates not only the discovery of incest but her own eventual fate, which is to become a nun. When Sebastian makes his attempt, it is not Almeyda who dissuades him but Dorax, who by then has indeed a chaste but burning love for his monarch, reviving the devotion of the dead Henriquez. Meanwhile, Almeyda's affection has become profoundly passionate love, in preparation for the linkage with death.

The most elaborate reversal of the play takes place between Dorax and Sebastian. In a tremendous debate near the end of Act IV, Sebastian recalls Dorax to his obedient service, invoking imagery of hell, damnation, and the fall of angels. In an equally tremendous debate in Act V, the imagery returns as Dorax rescues Sebastian from the sin of self-murder; the "converted" king says,

O thou has giv'n me such a glimpse of Hell,
So push'd me forward, even to the brink,
Of that irremeable burning Gulph,
That looking in th'Abyss, I dare not leap.
And now I see what good thou meanst my Soul,
And thank thy pious fraud: Thou has indeed,
Appear'd a Devill, but didst an Angells work.
(V, 526–32)

In the course of their highly charged debate, Dorax also picks up the imagery Sebastian had used in making the same case with Almeyda; but he transforms the "starless nights" into "black voluptuous slumber," in which Sebastian could figuratively keep his beloved always in his arms (V, 512–13)—an image uniting the dissolution of sexual climax and that of death.

Sexual passion, religious zeal, and political loyalty are thus forced together in the rhetoric and conduct of the three main characters. At the beginning of Act V there is a moment of explicitly Edenic rejoicing, when it looks as if the issues connected with these motifs are fortunately resolved. Almeyda is settled on her throne; the pious Sebastian seems blessedly married to his Christian bride; their loyal courtiers surround them. The apparent resolution is, however, mere Sophoclean irony; for all the horrors are unleashed in the denouement with its revelation of incest.

The joyful imagery of creation and paradise might suggest the delight of the English royal court (10 June 1688) at the blessing bestowed on James II and his bride when the Prince of Wales was born—a joy that gave way to despair as the daughter of the king turned against her father, while her husband successfully invaded England, and the royal family fled into exile—a year before Dryden's play was produced. Perhaps it was this inversion of the natural order, with England's political leaders playing renegade, her bishops joining the usurper, and her people rejecting their monarch, that underlay the disgust and disorder evoked by the imagery of *Don Sebastian*.

The play also seems to recall the motifs of *The Conquest of Granada*, though in a mood of cynicism. On several counts Sebastian and his darling Almeyda are like Almanzor and Almahide. Almahide forbids Almanzor to kill himself, and he rejects her offer of sisterly tenderness (part 1, V, i, 411–12, 448–53). In both plays the lovers yearn for the purely voluptuous ecstasy of sexual passion. The conflict of Christianity and Mohammedanism is central to both, keeping the lovers apart, yet bringing them together. In *The Conquest of Granada*, as in *Don Sebastian*, the heroine surrenders a throne while securing the hero.[14]

I think Dryden implicitly invites us to compare the fate of ideal, uncompromising heroism in the plays. With *Don Sebastian* he seems to contemplate for a last, miserable time the ideal which he had ambiguously recommended twenty years before. In *The Conquest of Granada*, Almanzor had represented a principle of unsullied, magnanimous will, admirable in itself, but unsuitable for a stable government. The hero discovered his true father in

14. In the end, of course, Almeyda regains her throne only to lose both it and Sebastian.

the Christian commander of the Christian king's troops, and himself joined the establishment of the Spanish monarch. Thus a warrior modeled on both Achilles and James II himself (as Duke of York) entered the service of a prudent ruler. At the end of *Don Sebastian*, when the young king decides to go into hiding, he leaves only an insignificant uncle to fill the throne of Portugal. His own chief officer Dorax unwillingly obeys the command of the abdicating monarch and remains in an impoverished world, mourning the loss of his ideal. We know that the historical Don Sebastian, who died in battle, left behind a party of supporters who hoped for his return as the English Jacobites hoped for that of James. If *The Conquest of Granada* alludes to the early career of James, *Don Sebastian* alludes to the later; for the battle of the royal hero on foreign soil, against an emperor who belongs to another religion, certainly points to the war between James II and William III in Ireland.[15]

The striking feature of Sebastian from our point of view is double. Unlike Almanzor he is not a hero of obscure origin challenging an order in power. He is himself an established monarch occupying his rightful throne, but at last renouncing it for a monastery. The reason is no conscious vice or crime, no lack of courage, piety, or great-heartedness, but the accident of unwittingly consummating a marriage with his own sister. The advantage of incest for the tragedian's purposes is that it happens to be among the very few horrifying, mortal sins which a Christian can commit in perfect ignorance, if only because he has been cut off from his sister or mother so early, so completely, and so long that he cannot identify her. This then is one of those crimes of love occasioned by "necessity or fatal ignorance" for which Dryden yearned as a means of insuring the pity of an audience for a royal, tragic hero.[16] It supplies a tragic flaw

15. Only James was in Ireland when the play was being completed; William went over, to head his fighting men, about half a year after the opening night.
16. Preface to *All for Love*; cf. John Loftis, *The Spanish Plays of Neoclassical England* (New Haven: Yale University Press, 1973), p. 245.

that does not weaken the moral authority of the protagonist. So we have a nearly perfect king who nevertheless gives up his kingship.

The long, last scene, in which Sebastian tries to end his life but is persuaded instead to obliterate himself from history, suggests a withdrawal from fact into myth. This effect is strengthened by Dryden's rhetoric and imagery, the association of sex with death, of life with penance, of royal power with sin. The reversals and symmetries of the action further stylize the quality of the play and help with the other elements to recall the ideal implications of the romance tradition, the regret that the world as it exists does not deserve a hero so exalted as Sebastian. Kingship, in Dryden's conception—true kingship—is too good for the English people. It is no longer a viable institution.

In *Don Sebastian*, therefore, Dryden says goodbye not merely to the heroism of romance and Almanzor, or to the ironical joys of nostalgia. He says goodbye to the very possibility of heroism, the idea itself. A world of bestiality and perverse sexuality, of renegade bishops and traitorous statesmen, can no longer bear the light of the values cherished by the poet. The king should be the fountain of honor. When Dryden implicitly suggests that monarchy in any valid form cannot survive the degeneracy of his countrymen, he treats the king's failure as a judgment against them, not him. For Dryden, it is not the exile who is impoverished; it is the world.

CHAPTER II

Swift: The Examiner and the Drapier

ֈ

Most people who read the weekly essays Swift wrote under the name of *The Examiner*[1] (in the years 1710–11) get a clear picture of the author as a political and social theorist. They observe that he believes the national constitution is twofold, comprising the Established Church as well as the machinery of state. They hear the Examiner's rhetoric linger on the excellence of monarchy as a form of government (Apr. 5, p. 125) and on the merits of the reigning queen, Anne. When he attacks the Whig party, they find him linking it to the idea of a democratic republic, accusing the Whigs of being anti-Christian (May 3, pp. 143–44), and associating their leaders with the lowest social classes. When he defends the Tory party, they find the Examiner attaching it to the old, titled families and to the gentry—i.e., the country gentlemen whose income was derived from large estates in land, which they had usually inherited and which they tried to enlarge by purchase and marriage.

Swift lines up the crown with the aristocracy, the gentry, the Church, and the Tories. He lines up the Whigs with the bankers, the stock jobbers,[2] and other forces supposed to be

1. *Prose Works*, III.
2. Cf. the references to the Bank of England and the East India Company (Apr. 19, p. 244).

resisting the crown. In religion the Examiner groups the Whigs with the sects and schools opposed to the Church of England: the Nonconformists (especially the Presbyterians), Deists, and atheists (May 3, p. 144).

These impressions of Swift's program do not mislead one. But I wish to qualify them by showing how many implications appear if we look closely at his language. For example, though he was a monarchist, Swift had an extraordinary imagination for the misdeeds and vices of kings. Writing in one *Examiner* about opinions falsely attributed to the Tories, Swift takes up the notion of unlimited obedience to a monarch. He denies that the Tories went nearly so far as the Whigs claimed. But to illustrate these false Whiggish claims, he indulges in prodigious suppositions of crimes a king might perpetrate:

> Though he should force [i.e., rape] your wife or daughter, murder your children before your face, or cut off five hundred heads in a morning for his diversion, you are still to wish him a long prosperous reign, and to be patient under all his cruelties, with the same resignation as under a plague or a famine; because to resist him would be to resist God in the person of his vice-gerent. If a king of England should go through the streets of London, in order to murder every man he met, passive obedience commands them to submit.... His next heir, though worse than what I have described, though a fool or a madman, has a divine undefeasible right to succeed him, which no law can disannul; nay though he should kill his father upon the throne, he is immediately king to all intents and purposes....
>
> (Mar. 22, p. 112)

The *Examiner* papers often praise Queen Anne, but few of the commendations are so vivid as these sarcastic fantasies. It is normal for an author of Swift's time to seem more vivid in fantasy than in describing things he has seen. Yet if one looks behind the eulogy of Anne as "a queen who engrosses all our love, and all our veneration" (Nov. 23, p. 20), one meets Swift giving lively instances of other sorts of rulers—like Edward II and Richard II, who lavished wealth and power on vicious favorites:

Whoever has been the least conversant in the English story [i.e., history] cannot but have heard of Gaveston, the Spencers, and the Earl of Oxford; who by the excess and abuse of their power, cost the princes they served, or rather governed, their crowns and lives. (Feb. 22, p. 93)

Meanwhile, in his most private letters, we discover Swift complaining that the queen is suspicious of the very men whom she ought to trust, and that she foolishly takes advice from some of the leading Whigs.[3] These biographical facts do not affect the meaning of Swift's arguments in *The Examiner*, but they alert us against exaggerating the implications of his vague praise. We may also notice that Swift himself had no good luck with royalty. At this time he could remember that William III never fulfilled a promise of preferment which Swift thought he had made. He could also see that the queen whom he celebrated showed no disposition to make his acquaintance or to encourage him. Yet his friends in power said they would introduce him to her majesty. (They never did.) If we look into the future, we may meet Swift calling her "a royal prude" in some verses resenting the failure to speed his advancement.[4]

Even in public, it was a delicate matter to eulogize her majesty. The ideal monarch, in Swift's exposition, must stand above both political parties and all social classes. In the *Examiner* papers, he magnified the royal prerogative and praised the queen as utterly devoted to the good of the nation. Yet the praise is subtly ambiguous. Swift does not want a case that rests on personal virtues. It must be constitutional. The Tories, he says, "prefer a monarchy before all other forms of government"; and the prerogative of the sovereign "ought, at least, to be held as sacred as the rights of his people" (Apr. 5, p. 232).

What Swift must recommend, therefore, is not her majesty alone as a virtuous individual but the hereditary, limited monarch as an essential part of lawful government. One reason he must do so is that Swift's campaign against the Whigs includes

3. *Journal to Stella*, Feb. 18 and Mar. 4, 1711.
4. "The Author upon Himself," line 1, *Poems*, I, 193.

the charge of favoring a republic (May 3, p. 142). They have, he says, "no great veneration for *crowned heads*"; and most of them "prefer a commonwealth before a monarchy" (Apr. 5, p. 123). This remark alludes to the rude treatment of Queen Anne by her abrasive friend Sarah, Duchess of Marlborough, and by Sarah's outspoken son-in-law, the Earl of Sunderland. To show off the Tories' better manners, and their idea of the constitution, the Examiner speaks of her majesty with reverence.

The awkwardness of Swift's attitude is that to hold his place rhetorically, he must avoid bringing in the predecessors of the queen or her probable successor. Her exiled father, James II, had to be condemned by Tory spokesmen because he had acted the part of a Roman Catholic tyrant subverting the Established Church (Apr. 12, pp. 235–36); and one of the Examiner's purposes was to cleanse his party of the dirt which its founders smeared on themselves when they supported the succession of James to the throne. So it was that Swift went out of his way to criticize James for his misgovernment (Apr. 12, pp. 235–37); and so it was that he accused the Whigs themselves of following James's policies (May 3, pp. 257–60).

The opposite problem arose from the example of Anne's brother-in-law, William III. The accession of the Dutch prince to the throne had agonized the Tories because it set aside both the reigning (or "abdicated") king and the Prince of Wales. William's ecclesiastical policy had alienated the Tories because he tried to strengthen the Dissenters. Besides, the Whigs treated William as their patron; and for Swift to place him in the foreground of a constitutional prospect would have confounded the Tories. The Examiner has harsh words for his reign (May 31, pp. 286–87).

Finally, the opinions of George of Hanover, who was the legal successor of the childless queen (after his mother's death), were only too well known. He could not be praised as a specimen of monarchy, because he was already working closely with the Whigs, and openly resented the foreign policy of Swift's friends.

We have only to remember that Swift's imagination normally operated better in satire than in eulogy; and we may then appreciate the implications of his pointed allusions to the possibility of royal misconduct. In a deep sense, although Swift considered monarchy the most practicable form of government for a nation like England, he had more reason to blame individual rulers of the country than to praise them. This ultimately is why his praise of monarchy had to be ambiguous. There was something paradoxical about his recommending an institution that was admirable in theory but troublesome in practice.

A related ambiguity touches Swift's effort to connect his friends' administration with ancient, titled families. A pearl, the Examiner said, might indeed be found on a dunghill, but that was not the first place where a man would look for one (May 10, pp. 266–68). Now it is true that her royal majesty's uncle, the Earl of Rochester, was Lord President of the Privy Council, and that the Duke of Buckingham was Lord Steward. But they could not match the aristocratic distinction of the Duke and Duchess of Somerset, who were the queen's Whig confidants; nor could they match the military splendor of the Duke of Marlborough, who had become at least publicly the hero of the Whigs. Since *The Examiner* regularly attacked both Marlborough and the arch-Whig Sunderland—whose family enjoyed conspicuous antiquity—it was a risky maneuver for Swift to blame the Whigs as hating the "ancient nobility."

It is more than a coincidence that the number of *The Examiner* in which Swift elaborated the importance of nobility is also the one in which he foretold the elevation of his friend Robert Harley, who was then the chief minister of the queen (May 10). Several features of the discussion must strike the well-informed reader. We know that Swift himself felt uneasy about Harley's preoccupation with genealogy, for he once said of him,

> As his own birth was illustrious, being descended from the heirs general of the Veres and the Mortimers, so he seemed to value that accidental advantage [i.e., high birth] in himself and others more than it could pretend to deserve.
>
> (*Prose Works*, VIII, 135)

But the truth was less palatable than Swift expressed it. Not only did Harley overvalue his connection with the de Veres and the Mortimers, but that connection did not exist. In no sense was Harley descended from either family.[5] Yet he took the de Veres' great title of Earl of Oxford when he became a peer, and he also saw to it that his claims were published in an absurd pamphlet in Latin and English.

This being so, one must smile at the implications of the last of the Examiner's paragraphs on the advantages of birth; for here Swift says,

> Nothing is more observable in those who rise to great place or wealth, from mean originals, than their mighty solicitude to convince the world that they are not so low as is commonly believed. They are glad to find it made out by some strained genealogy, that they have some remote alliance with better families.   (May 10, p. 151)

Did Swift realize how closely this insight touched his grand friend? I don't know. But I think it implies Swift's uneasiness about his own praise of noble families.

In *The Examiner*, Swift's aristocratic bias emerges from a double impulse: his respect for established families and his contempt for men promoted to high places from humble backgrounds. "The fortune of war," he complained, "hath raised several persons up to swelling titles, and great commands over numbers of men" (Dec. 21, p. 128).[6] When Swift means to belittle the men whom the Whigs brought into power, he says, "[The] lowest plebeians rise to the head of affairs, and there preserve themselves by representing the nobles and other friends to the old government, as enemies to the public" (Jan. 18, p. 153). As a party, the Whigs strengthen themselves—if we believe *The Examiner*—"by dependents raised from the lowest of the people" (Mar. 8, p. 205).

Of course, this line of attack was no more secure than the

5. *The Complete Peerage*, ed. G. E. Cokayne et al., 2nd ed. (London: St. Catherine Press, 1910–50), X, 264, note c.

6. Cf. the complaint of Sir Walter Elliot, in Jane Austen's *Persuasion*, about obscure persons rising through the navy (p. 19).

praise of aristocracy. The Tories possessed an ample share of plebeians. Their brilliant diplomat Matthew Prior had started his career by working in a tavern kept by an uncle. Harley's pet bishop, John Robinson, who became Keeper of the Privy Seal, sprang from an origin almost as humble. The most dramatic example of Swift's double view of ancestry is his treatment of Lord Somers, the gray eminence of Whiggery. In *The Examiner* Swift sneered at Somers for being derived from "the dregs of the people" (Feb. 1, p. 78). But in the dedication of *A Tale of a Tub*, seven years earlier, Swift not only described Somers as "the sublimest genius of the age, for wit, learning, judgment, eloquence and wisdom"; he also ridiculed supposititious flatterers who might take a genealogical tack and exalt his lordship's ancestry by tracing his pedigree "in a lineal descent from the House of Austria."

It would be only too easy to root Swift's ambiguity in his career. An Irish background was no blessing for a man with Swift's ambitions; and we may suppose he felt uneasy about his own lack of distinguished forebears, especially on his mother's side (*Prose Works*, V, 191–92). He may well have felt eager to bathe himself in the social brilliance of great courtiers.

Nevertheless, the opposite movement, though subdued, is also visible. I mean the Examiner's alignment with trade (not finance) and with the common people. In *The Examiner* Swift offers economic arguments against continuing the War of the Spanish Succession. He explicitly acknowledges the importance of trade. He puffs Harley for establishing a company to trade with Latin America (Jun. 7, pp. 295–96). As for his contempt for the common people, he mingles that with a respect for their judgment.

Although the Examiner often berates the Whigs for standing on the support of moneylenders and stockjobbers, he almost never identifies their faults with a peculiarly commercial (as against financial) tie. Once, in attacking the Whigs' large notions of religious toleration, he blames them for yoking that with trade; and he complains, "[These] men come with the spirit of shopkeepers to frame rules for the administration of king-doms; or, as if they thought the whole art of government con-sisted in the importation of *nutmegs*, and the cure of *herrings*" (Dec. 28, p. 48). But Swift limits his meaning at once by con-ceding that "trade and manufactures do always indeed deserve the best encouragement" (p. 49). It is the so-called "moneyed" men, or financiers, and not the merchants or tradesmen, whom the Examiner conscientiously denounces.

Toward the common people (variously defined) Swift shows his usual mixture of attitudes. As the riotous mob, they are invariably condemned, quite in the style of Dryden. So Swift blames their churlishness for the invention of party labels. The "vulgar," he says, "not troubling themselves to examine through the merits of a cause, are consequently the most violent partisans of what they espouse; and in their quarrels, usually proceed to their beloved argument of *calling names*" (May 31, p. 162). Their riotous temper pushes them to the front in great political changes; for these, Swift says, "have the same effect upon commonwealths that thunder has upon liquors, making the dregs fly up to the top" (Jan. 18, p. 65).

But "the people" may also refer to the mass of honest En-glishmen outside the institutions of government or church, and not belonging to the peerage, gentry, or upper bourgeoisie. As such—yeomen, artisans, shopkeepers, etc.—they receive frequent praise. Swift says they intuitively know the best interests of their country; he boasts that his friends in power have *vox populi* on their side (Jun. 7, p. 292); and he cheerfully agrees with Machiavelli that "the people, when left to their own judg-ment, do seldom mistake their true interests" (Jan. 18, pp. 64–65). Contrariwise, Swift says, if it is a Whig principle to appeal to the people, "that is only when they have been so wise as to poison their understandings beforehand" (Mar. 8, p. 105).

So far, I have been talking about prominent themes of the *Examiner* papers, and Swift's ambiguous attitude toward them. But Swift's power resides of course not in ambiguity. It is irony that raises his treatment of such themes into powerful rhetoric. To understand how he accomplishes the transformation, one must begin with his habit of lining up properties along the divisions of an issue. In the political debate, for instance, Swift fixes a fairly specific set of faults on the Whigs and sets these against matching virtues on the side of the Tories. The Whigs are restless and heterogeneous; the Tories are stable and homogeneous. The Whigs are corrupt and avaricious; the Tories are honorable and generous. The Whigs are insolent; the Tories, courteous.

Having created a system of contraries, Swift can rise to irony merely by praising the enemy for a quality he conspicuously lacks, or by blaming him for an absent virtue. A good example is a passage in which he goes down the list of Whig leaders, to show how their followers have endowed them with precisely those merits which *The Examiner* condemns them for ignoring. Marlborough here has liberality and gratitude; his wife has humility and gentleness; the licentious, anticlerical Earl of Wharton has piety and justice (Feb. 1, p. 77).

In dealing with the grandest persons, simply a lack of unction can fill an ironical remark with significance. Discussing a figure like Marlborough, who usually received the most respectful attention,[7] Swift has only to speak of him in casual or offhand language to diminish him and evoke ridicule. When the Examiner coolly writes that "excessive avarice in a general, is, I think, the greatest defect he can be liable to, next to those of courage and conduct," his tone itself brings Marlborough down to the level of mere mortals and washes out the lustre of military heroism (Feb. 22, p. 96).

We need not go further into Swift's habit of implying meanings through irony. If any aspect of his style is appreciated, this is. The emphasis remains correct, of course. But by dwelling on it, critics have obscured the true richness of the style. Even irony could not by itself give Swift his strength and depth. It is because his brilliant manner—he has plain manners too—is abundantly figurative that it dazzles the reader. Swift's irony invades the other tropes and figures, charging them with ridicule.

7. Swift himself comments on the fact (Nov. 23, p. 94).

Conventionally, figurative language works to dignify its subject; the sublime style normally abounds in figures. But Swift takes figures associated with elevation and inverts them. He employs ironical metaphors, similes, personifications, synecdoches, and allegories which implicitly degrade their subjects. No example is more obvious than the series of conceits in *A Tale of a Tub* comparing wisdom to a fox, a cheese, a sackposset, a hen, and a nut (*Prose Works*, I, 40).

In *The Examiner*, even on the level of mere similes, Swift's farfetched inventions are triumphant. One shining example is an association of the Whigs with war and revolution. To make this connection vivid and absurd at once, Swift finds an explosively compact conceit, comparing the Whigs to a sideshow at Bartholomew Fair, in which a girl balances swords on her hands and shoulders while turning around quickly:

> [The] Whigs owe all their wealth to wars and revolutions; like the girl at Bartholomew-Fair, who gets a penny by turning round a hundred times, with swords in her hands.
>
> (May 3, p. 147)

This kind of mock-conceit is hardly a method of implication; for the overt statement is part of the effect. But the ironical use of synecdoche goes further. Having associated disgraceful individuals and sinister cliques with the Whigs—as the heterogeneous ingredients of their party—Swift then takes any one person or group to stand for the whole congeries. Of course, instead of choosing an ennobling element, as the partisans themselves would prefer, he picks a shameful one and then expresses the figure ironically, seeming to praise where he really blames. Thus after establishing that the dissenting sects are among the constituent bodies of the Whig party, Swift first treats them as equivalent to the party as a whole. Then he reverses the connection ironically, making Presbyterianism (for instance) not a religious sect at all but a political faction. So he calls the Dissenters "the most spreading branch of the Whig party, that professeth Christianity" (Apr. 12, p. 234). Or else he says the Earl of Wharton "is a Presbyterian in politicks, and an atheist in religion, but he chuses at present to whore with a Papist" (*Prose Works*, III, 179). As implication the device is again unsubtle, but the cumulative ingenuity disarms criticism.

On the other hand, Swift's ironical use of personification is both subtle and radiant with suggestion. At its best this technique depends on a series of procedures. First Swift takes an abstract idea, probably of a vice. Then he personifies this and associates it with a person or group. For instance, in one *Examiner* paper Swift personifies the idea of merit and gives it a genealogy. Characteristically, he also produces false merit, a brother, who is often mistaken for true. In the context, true merit reaches toward the Tories, false merit toward the Whigs. Now Swift can say,

> [False] Merit filled the anti-chambers with a crew of his dependants and creatures, such as projectors, schematists, occasional converts to a party, prostitute flatterers, starveling writers, buffoons, shallow politicians, empty orators, and the like.
> (Mar. 1, p. 99)

Obviously, False Merit is a minister of state who acts as a patron of corrupt Whigs; and if Swift failed to make this fact explicit, few readers would not grasp it for themselves.

The highest refinement of ironical personification is to connect an ugly abstraction so regularly with an object of one's satire that at last the mention of the vice alone will be equivalent to the proper name of the victim. This is what Swift does with avarice or ambition, and the Duke of Marlborough.

He begins by blaming Marlborough for his desire to possess regal power and his love of money. For one *Examiner* paper Swift invents a letter to Marcus Crassus, the triumvir of ancient Rome, describing him in terms that point at the Duke of Marlborough. In the letter, with no irony, he scolds Crassus for covetousness. In later numbers of *The Examiner* Swift returns to the accusation, coupling it with the vice of inordinate ambition. He also goes on to write about the immaterial honors bestowed on his own friend Robert Harley, and Swift contrasts these pure rewards of virtue with mercenary compensation, saying that such true honors make a coin which "the receiver [knows] how to value, although neither *Avarice* nor *Ambition* would be able to comprehend its worth" (Mar. 29, p. 120). We may infer that by invoking the personified Avarice and Ambition, the author is contrasting the treacherous Duke of Marlborough with the honorable Robert Harley.

The ultimate stage soon follows. All Swift has to do is to pair Avarice off with Ambition, and the reader recognizes Marlborough in the personification. Writing about the danger to a monarch of tolerating insults from his favorites, Swift says that such a prince should extricate himself the moment he has the power, "because, from the monstrous encroachments of exorbitant Avarice and Ambition, he cannot tell how long it may continue to be so" (Apr. 19, p. 133).[8] The reader easily knows that the reference is to Queen Anne and Marlborough. In the very next number of *The Examiner*, Swift can drop the figure of speech altogether, and simply mention a set of politicians accustomed to power, who forget to be cautious "by excess of Avarice and Ambition." The implications of the apparently simple statement are obvious (Apr. 26, p. 139). Irony and the figure of personification are no longer wanted to alert us.

Of course, in his brilliant style, Swift does not keep the various devices apart but mingles them for cumulated energy. To show how he accomplishes this mingling, I shall use the attack on Wharton in *The Examiner* for November 9. Here the humblest stratum is the ironical pretense of celebrating his lordship for a talent which Swift naturally despises, viz. the knack of telling lies. But besides using praise for blame, Swift also indulges in a kind of allegory or parallel history; for instead of naming Wharton, he describes him in terms of Milton's Satan. This higher strain has to sustain yet another, because, by a kind of synecdoche, Swift makes Wharton alone stand for the whole Whig party. Finally, the surface of the argument is an elaborate personification. Swift purports to be writing not about an individual but about an abstraction, the art of political

8. Cf. Pope's treatment of Molly Skerrett as Vice in the *Epilogue to the Satires*, I, lines 141–48 (*Poems*, IV, 308–9).

lying. He pretends to give the history of this art but does so in language which applies either to the Whig party or to Wharton himself.

When one puts all the ingredients together, the suggestive force grows immense. The figures lure us into agreeing implicitly that every Whig is an atheist and a liar, that Satan was the first Whig, that all Wharton's crimes are typical of his entire party, that the Tories are quintessentially religious, patriotic, honest, etc. The essay is one of Swift's great successes, and yet it is only one of several in a series of remarkably high quality.

If I have been so far absorbed by the stylistic brilliance of the *Examiner* papers, I must now suggest why they receive little attention except from historical scholars. The reason, I think, is that Swift's best writing depends on a passionate moral idealism, and that the arguments he had to employ in *The Examiner* ran against that deep current. In the largest sense he was here attacking a false concept of heroism—that is, military heroism, narrowly national, unrelated to morality, unrelated to spiritual purpose. He was exploding a false kind of imperialistic glory feeding on the last stages of the War of the Spanish Succession, when a noble resistance to the aggression of Louis XIV had become an elementary greed for French territories and commerce.

To such false heroism he could have opposed either true heroism (in his terms, self-sacrifice for a high cause) or national prudence: both self-sacrifice and self-preservation were essential principles of Swift's genius. Unfortunately, it was national prudence that determined his rhetoric in *The Examiner*. Swift loathed war as an instrument of policy. He disliked standing armies and scoffed at the fame of soldiers. He also dreaded financial instability in the nation even as in his household. During the years 1710–1714 the great need of Swift's friends in power was to terminate a conflict that had lasted in effect for almost twenty-five years. When Swift advanced their peace efforts with his journalism, he went over and over the financial consequences of the war for Britain, and raised the question whether the stunning achievements of Marlborough's army were worth the enormous waste of lives and money that they entailed. At the same time, he denounced those statesmen who backed the war. They prolonged it, he said, for the bribes and perquisites that made them rich. To Marlborough above all Swift assigned the ugly role of preferring solid gold to immaterial honor.

The trouble with this depreciation of familiar ideals is that Swift had no generous aspirations to offer in their place. National prudence rarely stirs moral depths. When a controversialist writes for a government in power and blames the opposition for rashness, he can hardly pour exalting intensities into the reader's soul. Swift could not rise above prudential goals because the support for the war had itself derived from high principle: internationalism, religious and political freedom, the cause of humanity. The brilliance of Swift's satire therefore offers a magnificent display of devices to rally one's own fellows, but no moral appeal that echoes in the ears of posterity.

In *The Examiner*, I think Swift's instincts were at odds with the caution of his implicit values. He felt ill at ease with an unheroic, prudential rhetoric; and that discomfort showed itself in the ambiguities I have discussed. That an ironist should play with ambiguities is only proper. But Swift does not in fact play with these; he merely lets them appear—sometimes in spite of himself. The reservations he felt about the monarchy, the aristocracy, and the gentry never come into ironic manipulation. His sympathy with the common people emerges as a debating point; his sympathy with merchants and tradesmen sounds like a concession (Dec. 28, p. 49). His stand against the Dissenters remains unqualified by an ideal of national harmony uniting a variety of interests.

Finally, there is the character of the Examiner. Although Swift loved games of impersonation, and did tease the readers of the paper by throwing out and taking back hints of the author's identity,[9] he never went very far with the device. The general effect is close to that of the traditional author's ethos.

9. E.g., Dec. 7, pp. 107–8.

Thus the Examiner insists on his objectivity and truthfulness. He affiliates himself with appropriate men and institutions. He shows himself to be witty and playful. But his personality as such is not—as formalist critics might say—foregrounded.

The reason is that in these papers Swift assumed the point of view of a particular social class while founding his arguments on a show of impartiality. The landed gentry were well known to be the mainstay of the Tory party; they were not given to literary subtleties; and as a social type they were often a butt of satire. One could not be ostentatious about belonging to the class and seriously declare that one was unprejudiced. Once or twice, Swift did imply that the Examiner was a country gentle-man.[10] But he never dared to indulge in his favorite device of raising and lowering a mask while his real face grinned at the spectator. If Swift had made a comic turn of being and not being a squire, he would have risked alienating the very people he was addressing, and he would have subverted his own rhetoric.

By suggesting the ambiguity of Swift's antitheses in *The Examiner*, I have tried to prepare a reader for what happened to those features in his greatest political essays. During the years 1724–25, Swift interrupted the composition of *Gulliver's Travels* to produce a series of pamphlets called *The Drapier's Letters*. In these he pretended to be a drapier, or retail dealer in cloth, with the initials M. B., which may stand for Marcus Brutus. The occasion of the pamphlets was a quarrel between the English government and the Irish people. Although Ireland had her own parliament, judges, and apparatus of administration, the government in England effectively ruled the sister nation. Constitutionally, there may have been two distinct kingdoms of equal rank, sharing the same monarch. In fact, Ireland endured something of the status of a colony. In many ways her government was a shadow government. Too many of her high officials, judges, and bishops were simply sent over from England.

Statesmen often rested the case for English authority upon an act called Poynings' Law—going back to the reign of Henry

10. E.g., Nov. 16, p. 87.

VII—according to which all Irish legislation had to be approved by the king and the Privy Council of England. That old statute gained new vitality from the Declaratory (or Dependency) Act passed by the British Parliament in 1720. According to this act, the House of Lords of Ireland could not serve as the court of last appeal for Irish litigation, because the British Lords retained that function; and—much worse—the British Parliament was declared to possess full authority to make laws for Ireland.

The long-smouldering resentment of the Irish against such arbitrary power led to the controversy which Swift entered with *The Drapier's Letters*. An English ironmaster named William Wood had received a patent under the crown empowering him to issue a large quantity of copper money for Ireland. Nobody in Ireland was consulted on the matter; and the manufacture of the coins was to be so carelessly supervised that Wood might increase their quantity and lower their quality at will. Fortunately, silver or gold money was the only legal tender, and copper coins were merely for convenience; so anybody who wished might reject them. Gradually, the whole range of Irish social classes, political parties, and religious sects united in protest against the patent. From the evidence we have, it looks as if some leaders of the opposition asked Swift to help them; and in February, 1724, he certainly began to do so, taking the pseudonym of M. B. Drapier.

I wish to consider the superiority of *The Drapier's Letters* to the *Examiner* papers in their methods of implication and their conception of heroism. Essentially, Swift uses the same methods he used before. But now, instead of merely attacking a false idea of heroism, he defines a true one. Instead of merely exposing ambiguities, he handles them ironically. No longer do Swift's antitheses stem from political slogans. They now represent nations and principles.

Swift embodies Ireland in the heroic drapier whose voice he assumes. He embodies England in the villainous William Wood. Having set up these opponents, Swift associates certain persons and qualities with each. The drapier is patriotic; Wood is mercenary. The Irish want liberty and justice; the English wish to impose slavery and injustice. The Irish parliament and privy council side with liberty and the drapier; the English privy council, with Wood and oppression. As for George I and his prime minister Walpole, Swift shifts them back and forth with delicious ambiguity. They could not approve of Wood's scheme, and yet they must have approved of it. Swift has it both ways as he alternates the official lies with hints of the obvious truth.

Inside his large frame, Swift plays with the social types that appeared in the *Examiner* papers: the nobility and gentry, the common people, and the rest. But now he makes cunning use of their contradictory implications. The basic method is to expose the absurd inconsistencies of the government's case by uttering officially approved propositions in a way that defies fact or probability. For example, it was well known that the Duke of Grafton as Lord Lieutenant of Ireland had approved of Wood's patent, and it was unreasonable to suppose that he would not have known about it. Yet for reasons of state his grace—a royal bastard and a booby—denied having intelligence of the matter. All the Drapier had to say was,

> But the *Late Lord Lieutenant of Ireland* affirmed it was a Secret to him (and who will doubt of his VERACITY, especially when he Swore to a Person of Quality; from whom I had it, that Ireland should never be troubled with these Half-pence).
> (*Drapier*, p. 47)

Nothing more is wanted to annihilate the character of a brainless figurehead.

The king himself receives far more elaborate treatment. He is theoretically above parties; he is the father of his people, whether Irish or English. As a king he must of course be handled with respect by any journalist. Swift therefore ostentatiously grants him the attributes of royalty and explicitly opposes him to the contemptible William Wood.

Along with such conventional reverence, however, Swift offers innuendoes. First, he refers so heavily to the monarch's kindness and to the loyalty of the Irish people that an attentive reader might wonder why his majesty's benevolence was not more effective, or why the Irish were so blindly loyal to their sovereign. In the *Third Letter* his implication becomes explicit; and the Drapier observes,

> His Majesty . . . is pleased to say that *He will do every Thing in his Power for the Satisfaction of his People.* It should seem therefore, that the Recalling of the Patent is not to be understood as a Thing *In his Power.*   (*Drapier*, p. 60)

The other innuendo depends on the central fact of law, that nothing but silver or gold is legal tender, and so consequently nobody need touch the copper money. Swift chooses to convey this crucial truth in references to the king, and to say repeatedly that his majesty, even if he wished to make people take the halfpence and farthings, could not do so. The possibility that the king might after all sink to such illegality grows inescapable, and the idea of the king is correspondingly discolored.

As the innuendoes press down, they crush the respectful allusions until every reference to "our GRACIOUS PRINCE"[11] or "his Sacred Majesty" [12] sounds ironical. One example will illustrate the general effect. Urging the people to reject Wood's coins, Swift tells them,

> It is no Treason to Rebel against Mr. WOODS. His MAJESTY in his Patent obliges no body to take these Half-Pence, our GRACIOUS PRINCE hath no such ill Advisers about him; or if he had, yet you see the Laws have not left it in the KING's Power, to force us to take any Coin, but what is Lawful, of right Standard *Gold* and *Silver*. . . .[13]

On the one hand, George I is "our gracious prince." On the other, if he imposed the coins on his Irish subjects, he would be breaking the law. Swift invites the reader to envisage a contradiction between kingship and justice.

The Drapier emits a remarkable number of allusions to the king, most of them casual and undignified—though in perfectly

11. Letter I, p. 14.   12. Letter II, p. 26.
13. Letter I, p. 14.

decent language. The actual words "king" and "majesty" occur about two dozen times in the first of *The Drapier's Letters*. Though none of these references is openly offensive, the cumulation makes one feel a conflict between the terms of deep respect and the easiness of the tone. Such a discord of theme and tone is a common ironic technique, much affected by Swift —I have indicated that the Examiner gave the treatment to Marlborough.

In his *Third Letter*, the Drapier says, "Surely his Majesty, when he consented to the Passing of this Patent, *Conceived* he was doing an Act of Grace to his Most Loyal Subjects of *Ireland*, without any Regard to Mr. *Wood*, farther than as an *Instrument*" (p. 45). By this time it hardly matters whether we fasten on the simple sense of the outburst, or the truthful, rational implication that the king never thought of serving his people. Either way, it becomes an indictment of George I.

So also Swift plays with the relation between Wood and the king. In the *First Letter* he observes that Wood got the patent ultimately from the crown but through advisers who misled his majesty. But he detaches Wood from the king, as an obscure culprit who has succeeded in a low, contemptible piece of iniquity. As the *Letters* go on, this relationship alters. Swift insinuates that the king might be in agreement with Wood's views. He even proposes ironically that Wood has usurped the royal prerogative and made himself an "arbitrary mock-monarch."[14]

One hears other hints that Wood has pre-empted the place of a king. The Drapier compares himself to John Hampden refusing to pay ship money, and thus casts Wood in the part of Charles I.[15] He describes the Master of the Royal Mint as if he works not for the crown but for Wood.[16] He speaks of Wood as "daring to prescribe what no King of England ever attempted"; and he also produces a ferociously climactic metaphor:

14. Letter II, p. 24.   15. Ibid., p. 25.
16. Ibid., p. 41.

It is no Loss of Honour to submit to the *Lyon*, but who, with the Figure of a *Man*, can think with Patience of being Devoured alive by a *Rat*.   (*Drapier*, p. 25)

Here Swift implies that King George has abandoned his responsibilities as father of his people and allowed Wood to act as an absolute tyrant. The lion himself has become a rat. It is notable that while fewer figures of speech occur in *The Drapier's Letters* than in *The Examiner*, those few have immense resonance.

If Swift could travel so far with a monarch, the same method of ambiguous antitheses carries him still further with the prime minister. For Walpole, the Drapier's gestures of respect are more perfunctory than for King George, and his insinuation of the minister's collaboration with Wood is bolder. The favorable language therefore quickly begins to sound sarcastic, and the heavy suppositions become implicit certainties. In the *Fourth Letter* the ambiguity of Swift's rhetoric carries us into the following sentence, which defies the reader's knowledge that no government business took its course without Walpole's backing; thanks to the great man's reputation for total corruption, the sentence is both logical and false, producing savage implications about the nature of government:

> But I will now demonstrate beyond all Contradiction that Mr. W—— is against the Project of Mr. *Wood*, and is an entire Friend to Ireland, only by this one invincible Argument, that he has the Universal Opinion of being a Wise Man, an able Minister, and in all his Proceedings pursuing the *True Interest* of the *King* his Master: And that as his Integrity is above all *Corruption*, so is his *Fortune* above all *Temptation*.
>
> (*Drapier*, pp. 86–87)

In other words, the interests of a king are opposed to those of his people; and no matter how rich a great minister may be, he will connive at crimes in return for bribes.

A parallel ambiguity affects the diatribe against Wood. Swift lingers on the contrast between the ironmonger's meanness and the magnitude of his lawless achievement. Endlessly, Swift defines the issue of the patent as a conflict between a single evildoer and a whole kingdom. And yet, we gather, Wood has his accomplices, and England herself stands behind him. So the horror of one negligible villain destroying a whole people evolves into the horror of a powerful, imperial nation stifling her weaker sister.

Openly, the Drapier denounces Wood as unutterably contemptible and solitary. Yet the knave is incredibly powerful at the same time, for he is capable of ruining Ireland. Now the meaner Wood appears, the harder it becomes to account for his triumph. Driven to locate an adequate cause of the enormity, the reader thinks metonymically of others, half-associated with Wood's career by the Drapier's argument. Finally, one must seek out the true contrivers in Walpole and King George. Meanwhile, those mighty persons in turn sink figuratively to the level of serving as tools of a despicable hardwareman. When, therefore, the Drapier openly denounces Wood, we infer that he is covertly denouncing the prime minister and the king.

Thus the old figures of metonymy and synecdoche abide in *The Drapier's Letters* as in *The Examiner*. But the differences are illuminating. One is that Swift vastly enlarges the scope of his own side by rising above the simple legality of the patent. Where the English privy council had agreed that the royal prerogative empowered his majesty to dispose as he pleased of the privilege of minting coins, the Drapier wonders whether the prerogative was not meant to be exercised for the benefit of the people. His postulate—*salus populi suprema lex*—was to remain valid, and to serve the American colonists against the great-grandson of George I.

We hear the Drapier refuse to allow statute law or the rule of precedents to justify the misdeeds of the English ministry. For such mere legalities he substitutes the ultimate sanctions, larger than any national code, on which the concept of justice must rely. By appealing to Lockean principles of natural law, he makes Ireland represent humanity as a whole, while the Drapier stands for liberty; and Swift foreshadows the appeal Burke was to make in his speech on conciliation with the American colonies:

The question with me [said Burke] is, not whether you have a
right to render your people miserable; but whether it is not
your interest to make them happy. It is not, what a lawyer tells
me I *may* do; but what humanity, reason, and justice tell me I
ought to do.[17]

Yet the force of *The Drapier's Letters* does not spring from
the mere elevation of Swift's views. It operates more subtly and
elaborately through the games Swift plays with the character
of the Drapier. It may be significant that personification is far
more rare in *The Drapier's Letters* than in *The Examiner*. I
suspect the reason is that Swift in the *Letters* makes so much
more use of impersonation. The identity of the Drapier is richer
by far than that of the Examiner, and it has a fundamental connection with Swift's ideals. The bumptious earthiness of the
Drapier gives solidity to the ideals, and the grandeur of the
ideals fills the character of the Drapier with heroic dignity. It
is not high principle alone or the rich identity by itself that
distinguishes the *Letters*. It is the interfusion of the two.

Swift's devices of impersonation are really a form of irony,
because one can analyze any deliberate irony into the acting of
a part. Socrates pretended to be an ignorant man when he prac-
ticed his peculiar form of inquiry, even as Swift puts on the
mask of naïveté for his satires. But the theatrical aspect shines
in the *Letters*. As the Drapier, Swift not only puts himself
forward but calls attention to certain of his traits and to some
quasi-biographical facts in ways that are attractively humorous
and dramatic. Unlike the Examiner, he hides and reveals himself provocatively, now as M. B., now as Swift. Like the Examiner's irony, the Drapier's playful self-exposure invades his
other rhetorical devices. Brilliant figures of speech drawn from
Scripture suggest the priestly character of the author even while
explicit features mark the person of a drapier.[18] From the start a

17. *Select Works*, ed. E. J. Payne, 2nd ed. (Oxford: Clarendon
Press, 1890), I, 196. Although American Revolutionary spokesmen sometimes echoed Swift's language, the ideas they invoked went back, of course,
to earlier political theorists.
18. Cf. in Letter III the reference to an illiterate shopkeeper (p. 36)
and the parallel with David (p. 63).

majestic figure, finally recognizable as the Dean of St. Patrick's, lowers behind the shopkeeper; and the meaning of his words alters as we listen to one voice or the other.

Unlike the Examiner, the Drapier becomes not merely a spokesman but a heroic defender. Activities that are humdrum in themselves take on epic grandeur when the great-hearted tradesman sets the example; and he is a hero whose boldness is untempered by affiliation with a winning party or a government in power. Rather, as in the *Third Letter*, Swift goes out of his way to show off the Drapier's single-handedness:

> I am very Sensible that such a Work as I have undertaken might have worthily employed a much better Pen. But when a House is attempted to be Robbed it often happens that the weakest in the Family runs first to stop the Door. All the Assistance I had were some Informations from an *Eminent Person*, whereof I am afraid I have Spoiled a Few by endeavouring to make them of a Piece with my own Productions, and the Rest I was not able to manage. . . .   (*Drapier*, p. 63)

By setting himself apart, the Drapier magnifies his heroism and directs our attention to the fact that Swift picked an humble shopkeeper for his disguise. One might suppose these turns were mere debaters' tricks if the *Fourth* and *Fifth Letters* did not show their implications for Swift's political and social philosophy. To clarify that significance, we may just glance at the relations between the Drapier and his audience, noticing how Swift plays with various social types.

In the original *Letter*, the Drapier spoke as a shopkeeper himself to the "shopkeepers, tradesmen, farmers, and common-people." The practical reason was, I assume, that the richer, better educated classes could be trusted to appreciate their rights and to refuse Wood's coins, while the humbler shopkeepers and tenant farmers might feel intimidated.[19] But whatever the cause, Swift was following the opposite tack to that of

19. Cf. Swift's remark in Letter VI: "If this Copper should begin to make it's way among the common, ignorant People, we are inevitably undone; it is they who give us the greatest Apprehension, being easily frighted, and greedy to swallow Misinformation" (p. 137).

The Examiner, and identifying himself with the lower social classes. This identification continued throughout the five letters published in the years 1724–25.

As a heroic member of their own order, the Drapier can express both sides of his feeling for the common people, his affectionate protectiveness and his angry contempt. Unlike the Examiner with the gentry, he need not ignore the ambiguity. So he cheers them on and chastises them by turns. They are innocent victims of English oppression, but they are also wicked betrayers of their own salvation.

> It is your Folly [the Drapier says] that you have no common
> or general Interest in your View, not even the Wisest among
> you, neither do you know or enquire, or care who are your
> Friends, or who are your Enemies.   (*Drapier*, p. 3)

The loving, scolding note is that of a father, teacher, priest. A reader might well wonder whether any simple shopkeeper could have the learning and penetration shown by the Drapier; and he might notice signs in the very first *Letter* that the true author was the notorious Dean Swift who had already risked his security for the good of Ireland.[20]

Finally, the reader might discover two attitudes, in this letter, toward the nobility and gentry, i.e., toward the great landowners whom Swift considered to be the natural rulers of a country. The Drapier takes their superiority for granted; the government and the economy, he suggests, rightly depend on them. Yet he complains bitterly that (unlike the common people) they waste the wealth of the nation in England—"a great Number of *Lords* and *Squires*, whose Estates are here, and are our Countrymen, spend all their *Lives* and *Fortunes* there" (p. 5).

As the *Letters* continue, these ambiguities deepen, along with the shifting attitudes toward Wood, Walpole, and the king; and as they deepen, the ironical implications ramify.

---

20. After praising the author of *A Proposal for . . . Irish Manufacture* (i.e., Swift), the Drapier says, "However I cannot but warn you once more . . . ," (p. 4), thus identifying himself as Swift.

In the *Second Letter* the rallying and reproaching of the common people continue, suggesting how comfortable the Drapier feels with them. He addresses the gentry and nobility with respect, and urges them to instruct their tenant farmers to refuse Wood's coins (pp. 29–31). But we also hear a caustic allusion to absentee landlords (pp. 27–28). Again, the Drapier makes much of his being a shopkeeper (p. 20), and yet speaks rashly, in the tones of a heroic champion risking his life for his country:

> . . . I will Shoot Mr. *Woods* and his Deputies through the Head, like *High-way Men* or *House-breakers*, if they dare to force one Farthing of their Coyn upon me. . . . (*Drapier*, p. 25)

In the *Third Letter* a movement begins that seems crucial for Swift's whole career. Not only does the Drapier dwell on his single-handedness as champion of the nation; he also hints at the inactivity of the governing classes (p. 63). Though addressing this pamphlet to the nobility and gentry, the Drapier carefully separates himself from them, repeatedly mentioning his own low condition (p. 35) as an "illiterate shopkeeper" (p. 36), poor, ignorant (p. 38), and mean (p. 44). For his climactic figure of speech, in a pamphlet that has several other Biblical allusions, he picks an Old Testament parallel comparing himself to David (p. 63), and generally, I think, hinting at a priestly speaker. One cannot miss the implicit complaint that the great men of Ireland felt reluctant to do battle with the Philistine while an illiterate shopkeeper became the champion of Israel. Even if one "eminent person" did assist him, the Drapier says,

> I was in the Case of *David* who *could not move in the Armour of Saul*, and therefore I rather chose to attack this *Uncircumcised Philistine* (*Wood* I mean) *with a Sling and a Stone*.
> (*Drapier*, p. 63)

Both as M. B. Drapier and as Dean Swift, the author prefers to belong to the people rather than to their betters.

A striking paradox of *The Drapier's Letters* derives from Swift's treatment of money. As in *The Examiner* he is connecting the preservation of a kingdom with financial prudence.

Why then does the later work seem so much loftier? First, Swift spiritualizes the theme. In his rhetoric the rejection of the coins sounds like self-sacrifice and self-preservation together. It is the English who exude avarice; it is they who scramble for pensions and sinecures (pp. 73–74); and it is Wood who sacrifices conscience to cash.

Contrariwise, it is the Irish who refuse to defile themselves with the filthy metal. The literal gesture becomes figurative as they turn their backs on money and embrace patriotism. (In *The Examiner*, profit and patriotism merge.) Swift also adds to the spiritual implications by using Biblical phrases and images to suggest the sinfulness of Wood's forces or the virtue of his own.

But Swift does much more by rooting the opposition to Wood's coins in the largest constitutional issues and the meaning of human freedom. The *Fourth Letter* is the one that fixes this enlargement, and it is here that Swift's reorientation grows clearly visible. Addressing the "whole people" of Ireland, the Drapier now implies that they must be ready to seize those rights which the tyrants in England have denied them. Force, he indicates, is the only sanction of an oppressive regime (pp. 79, 85–86); and if such a government ignores the needs and wishes of its subjects, it deserves—by this reasoning—no loyalty.

Swift's high-mindedness becomes cogent because the Drapier sets the example for his audience: he himself offers to answer English injustice with violence (p. 79). But by the same token he disregards an overwhelming counterargument; for the rulers of Ireland—the Anglican landowners—could keep their power (in a country where they comprised a fractional minority) only with the backing of British troops. Constantly, the government in Westminster had to be ready with military force which it might bring to bear in Ireland against the mass of Roman Catholics of native stock. Otherwise, the social order to which Swift himself belonged would collapse, and the church he served would shrivel up.

Simply ignoring this truth, Swift denounces the view that Ireland is a "depending kingdom." "All government without the consent of the governed," he declares, "is the very definition of slavery" (p. 79). "By the laws of God, of nature, of nations, and of your own country," he tells the Irish, "you are and ought to be as free a people as your brethren of England" (p. 80).

Fifty years later, these sentiments might nourish the American colonists. But the Irish nobility and great landlords would hardly associate themselves with such language. The doctrines the Drapier taught, if truly applied, would have undone the property settlement of Ireland.

He was equally alarming in his treatment of the king. Taking up the royal prerogative to coin money, the Drapier opens with a rational, fatherly tone and humble language. He shows how narrowly the king's independent authority is limited. But instead of being gingerly, he goes on to sound almost insolent when he explains yet once more that no British monarch may compel his subjects to take coin other than sterling or gold. In effect, the Drapier defines the prerogative so nakedly that no officer of the government could publicly agree with him:

> But we are so far from disputing the King's *Prerogative* in Coyning, that we own he has Power to give a Patent to any Man for setting his Royal Image and Superscription upon whatever Materials he pleases, and Liberty to the Patentee to offer them in any Country from *England* to *Japan*, only attended with one small Limitation, That *no body alive is obliged to take them.* (*Drapier*, p. 70)

It is not surprising that such language scared leaders in the Drapier's camp. Swift had transformed himself from an aide into a manipulator of those who were resisting the patent. The *Letter to the Whole People* represented his own policy, not his service to another man's program. Among the high legal officers—Chief Justice Whitshed, Chief Baron Hale, and Attorney-General Rogerson (the first and last being Irish by birth and education)—all agreed that the *Fourth Letter* was "a seditious and vile libel, and fit to be prosecuted." The Chancellor himself was Lord Midleton, son of a Cromwellian officer who had received a large grant of Irish land. Midleton thought the *Fourth*

Letter was "highly seditious," and that the author and printer deserved to be punished, or at least he said so to the Lord Lieutenant.[21] Yet Midleton also opposed Wood's patent.

When the Privy Council of Ireland met to condemn the *Fourth Letter*, only one of the twenty-one members present voted against the motion. When they divided on proclaiming a reward for the discovery of the author, only four members voted against the motion.[22]

No wonder the Drapier revealed some reservations in his identification with the whole people. As we move from the *Fourth* to the *Fifth Letter*, we cannot ignore Swift's change of allegiance, or the fact that he no longer assumes that simply as property holders, the nobility and great landowners are the proper rulers of the kingdom. It becomes supremely important now that Swift should wear the mask of a shopkeeper. Unlike the Examiner, the heroic Drapier does not tie himself to a class or a ministry.

Swift signalized a break with his old allies by addressing his *Fifth Letter* to Lord Molesworth, an anticlerical Whig whom Swift's friend Harley had once turned out of the Privy Council of Ireland. Robert Molesworth had made himself conspicuous for two principles which the government could have wished at this time to be mutually exclusive: a concern for the welfare of Ireland and a loyalty to Whig traditions and the House of Hanover. Although in matters of religion Swift set Molesworth among the damned, in political economy he found his lordship's zeal angelic. Molesworth's *Considerations for Promoting Agriculture* (1723) delivered useful hints of the same tendency as Swift's own program. The dedication of that pamphlet could only have completed the reversal of Swift's attitude toward Molesworth. It was inscribed to the Irish House of Commons in recognition of their brave union against Wood's patent; and here Molesworth eulogized the votes of the Commons as

21. See his letter of Oct. 31, 1724, in William Coxe, *Memoirs of the Life and Administration of Sir Robert Walpole* (London, 1798), II, 396–97.

22. *Drapier*, pp. xliv–xlv.

an eminent instance of your wisdom and love to your country, in your just censure and vigorous resolutions against a patent calculated to destroy your trade, rob you of your money; and which calls you slaves and fools to your faces.[23]

The implicit meaning of dedicating the *Fifth Letter* to Molesworth becomes clear when one fits his lordship into the set of antitheses that Swift had established.[24] By tracing his own allegedly wicked expressions to a man whom the king delighted to honor, the Drapier confounded the royal ministers and infused confidence into their opponents. Cutting across outworn distinctions, his arguments drew on a principle that combined Christian charity (or benevolence) with eminent practicality, a principle illuminated by the appeal to Molesworth.

This is the idea of productivity. In the scheme of polarities which the Drapier used to divide those who backed Wood's patent from those who fought it, Swift finally linked not only justice but productivity with the opposition. Even during his discussion of political freedom, he would leave the immediate controversy behind, and make the issue of the patent simply an entry into the larger subject of Ireland's economic welfare. In that very great matter he implicitly set the productive landowners, farmers, manufacturers, and tradesmen against the parasites and drones: the absentee landlords, the idle pensioners, the government officers—the tribe of mercenary English opportunists who not only failed to perform the jobs they were paid for but even stepped out of their way to injure the country that fed them. Eventually, Swift would be tempted to exclude the resident landlords themselves from the productive body because of their irresponsibility, oppressiveness, and greed; but that was a turn he was not yet ready to take.

If one keeps in mind this implicit distinction between productive and unproductive men, the word "people" may have at least two senses. One is the "true English" minority to

---

23. Quoted in Oliver W. Ferguson, *Swift and Ireland* (Urbana: University of Illinois Press, 1962), p. 81.

24. It becomes quite explicit in Letter VII, pp. 146, 151, 156, 158–60, 169, 171–72.

which Swift belonged: the Anglican descendants of English families who had come over and taken possession of the country. The other is the nobility, farmers, artisans, and so forth who lived in the kingdom and contributed to its prosperity. Certainly, those whom the Drapier tried to combine against Wood's patent included Roman Catholics and Presbyterians.

So it seems fair to say that Swift's arguments brought all the productive and public-spirited men of Ireland together in a bloc defying the oppressors of their country. The boundaries between Whig and Tory, High Church and Low Church, no longer concern the Dean of St. Patrick's (though he was to revert to them repeatedly and bitterly in controversies of church and state). A greater principle, the salvation of the people, has transcended them.[25]

I think it no accident that in this *Fifth Letter* Swift made the most of his old game of masks, flaunting the pretense that the author is a drapier, and making an allegory of his autobiography. In a series of paragraphs devoted to this transparent impersonation, Swift reviews his career as an Irish patriot by talking about his pamphlets as if they were pieces of cloth. Speaking of the success of the *Third Letter*, he says,

> This incited me so far, that I ventured upon a *Fourth* Piece made of the best *Irish* Wooll I could get, and I thought it Grave and Rich enough to be worn by the best *Lord* or *Judge* of the Land. But of late some *Great Folks*[26] complain as I hear, that when they had it on, they felt a *Shuddering in their Limbs*, and have thrown it off in a Rage, cursing to Hell the poor *Drapier* who invented it, so that I am determined never to *work for Persons of Quality* again, except for your *Lordship* and a *very few more*.   (*Drapier*, p. 103)

When the game of impersonation erupts in this pamphlet, Swift treats his various past performances in the Irish interest as due to separate authors, and he even mentions conversations which the Drapier had with a certain "Dean," who is of course Swift. Few readers would not have known that the Dean and

25. This implication becomes explicit in Letter VII, pp. 161–63.
26. I.e., Whitshed and the Privy Council of Ireland.

all these authors were one and the same person. The effect of the transparent disguises is to imply the danger of the Drapier's work and his insouciance in meeting it. But Swift also implies that while the single, heroic, humble patriot did the job of a multitude, the men of rank refused to take any risk for the sake of their nation.[27]

If we look beyond the five letters published in 1724 and 1725, I think we shall find Swift staying on course. In a *Drapier's Letter* composed in 1725 but only published ten years later, he went over a number of practical measures for improving the Irish economy even within the grotesque limits set by England. Here Swift gave concentrated attention to the irresponsibility of the nobility and gentry who lived and spent their income abroad (pp. 158–60); and he ended the whole essay with a sentiment which was to be echoed by the King of Brobdingnag:

> And I shall never forget what I once ventured to say to a great Man in *England*; That few *Politicians*, with all their Schemes, are half so useful Members of a Commonwealth, as an *honest Farmer*; who, by skilfully draining, fencing, manuring and planting, hath increased the intrinsick Value of a Piece of Land. . . . (p. 172)

The identification of productiveness with virtue, and Swift's sympathy with the common people, led to a further turn when he acknowledged that the landlords themselves were to blame for the misery of the kingdom. A few years after writing the *Drapier's Letters*, Swift produced *A Modest Proposal*, in which not the English government but the feckless Anglican gentry of Ireland found themselves condemned as butchers of their fellow countrymen. Still later, in one of his last and most savage poems, *The Legion Club*, Swift denounced the irresponsibility of that very House of Commons which he had celebrated as the Drapier and which was the organ by which the gentry (along with the nobility) governed the country.

It would not be hard to show that Swift's sympathy with the common people deepened during this same period. But I

27. "I look upon my self, the *Drapier*, and my numerous Brethren, to be all true Patriots in our several Degrees" (Letter VI, p. 141).

shall offer only one rather moving piece of evidence. In the original form of the *Fifth Letter*, the Drapier spoke of "the rabble" as being eager to destroy images of William Wood. For the 1735 edition of his works, Swift emended the expression from "rabble" to "my faithful Friends the Common People" (*Drapier*, p. 110n).

CHAPTER III

Pope: Bipolar Implication

✤

Near the source of Pope's work is an anxiety understandable in terms of his health and religion. As a Roman Catholic in a Protestant nation, Pope suffered maddening penalties. He could not attend a university or hold a civil office. He paid double the normal tax on land, and the law forbade him to reside within ten miles of London. All Roman Catholics were exposed to charges of conspiring against the government.

But Pope's worst affliction was tuberculosis of the spine, which gave him rickets and a progressive, lopsided curvature of the back. It made him grotesquely short and gradually weakened his thin limbs. It produced much languor, a susceptibility to bad colds, and other painful or unpleasant symptoms which worsened as he aged. Pope had to wear a stiff corset, warm clothes, and (over the skinny legs) three pairs of stockings. Normal sexual relations were out of the question.

Frail, vulnerable, and (in effect) impotent, it was natural for the poet to desire the security of well-placed friends. One of the mainsprings of his imagination was the need to protect himself. Still he was conscious of his genius and wanted fame. He yearned to exercise heroic power over others through the gift of poetry.

To gain the recognition he longed for, Pope had to mask many emotions. As an adolescent, he began a career of seeking out men of talent, rank, or power, winning their friendship and making them serve him. To do so, he learned to charm them with tact and wit, paying careful compliments and accommodating himself to the moods of the mighty.

Not only in his poems but also in his letters and conversation, Pope systematically maintained careful representations of himself that would uphold an appearance of strength, independence, and natural benevolence, all in keeping with the doctrines he recommended in verse. What records we have of his conversation suggest that he hoped his sentiments would be repeated. The rhetoric of Pope's most familiar letters sometimes sounds like that of a senator emitting platitudes for his own obituary. A second reader—Posterity—normally looked over the poet's epistolary shoulder.

I assume that these constraints, added to those of health and religion, nourished a deep resentfulness which compounded the original anxiety. The poetic instinct bent itself to please those whom Pope needed, while the very impulse to create started from subterranean discomforts. Words are a common resource of those who cannot act, but Pope's words had many duties. They vented painful emotions which the poet dared not express simply. They conveyed an air of assurance to cloak a fundamental unease. They made up for a lack of sexual authority. They rewarded friends and punished enemies.

Pope devised methods of attracting and reassuring those who might be hostile to his brilliance, and yet of challenging subtle readers by offering them dangerous thoughts. Wit and irony are known ways of accomplishing these ends, and good critics have examined Pope's use of them. He found other ways as well, which are less familiar.

If we agree that sex, religion, and politics are themes which invite indirection, we may also agree that religion, for Pope, was too risky a subject to experiment with. He did venture on opinions that might trouble his coreligionists, especially a tolerance of non-Catholic positions. He blamed great ecclesiastics for time-serving, avarice, and other vices. But he did not indulge in satire on allegedly false doctrines, as Dryden and Swift had done. In *The Messiah* and *An Essay on Man*, Pope tried, explicitly and implicitly, to avoid controversy.

Sexual themes were treacherous too. The poet's obvious incapacity drove him to adopt conventional poses for fear of becoming too easy a mark for ridicule. Whether he used a rake or a moralist as his mouthpiece, he could hardly afford to sound innovative. Yet if sexual themes particularly excite wordplay, they must have exerted a special charm upon a poet. Pope felt the charm, and characteristically offered both conformist and subversive treatments of those themes.

The association of sexuality with creative power is natural. Keeping this connection in mind, one must notice Pope's tendency to maintain it and yet to separate the imagery of conception from that of sexual intercourse. He liked to refer to his works as his progeny and to the muse as a wife, but not to lovemaking between the creative pair.

In these misty crossings we touch the depths of Pope's identity. He offered several distinct representations of the poetic character. The most familiar is the public idealization of an uncorrupt spokesman for patriotic and social virtue. This is the character he liked to give his own career. Yet implicitly, the ideal public figure depreciates another, viz. the inspired artist celebrated by Horace and recommended by Pope in *An Epistle to Augustus*:

> 'Tis he, who gives my breast a thousand pains,
> Can make me feel each passion that he feigns,
> Inrage, compose, with more than magic art,
> With pity, and with terror, tear my heart.
>
> (lines 342–45)

In these lines "poet" clearly means seductive playwright rather than didactic satirist.

But there is still another figure, for which Pope voices contempt and which he embodies in the persons of failed or inept authors. This alas is the one that excites his greatest energy, his most imaginative language. Therefore, although it alludes normally to writers whom Pope disliked, one may speculate that it also reflects Pope's doubts about his status. He might be a uniquely gifted genius; but putting aside traditional hyperboles, what did the laurel crown amount to when it topped his crazy carcass?

So one may also speculate about the scenes of grotesque fantasy that break out in Pope's best work. Underground, cavernous, and obstetric images, tinged with sexuality, suggest that literary parenthood compensated the poet for the loss of voluptuous pleasure. Pope designed deeply coherent masterpieces around heroines deprived of normal sexual relations: *Eloisa to Abelard, An Elegy to . . . an Unfortunate Lady* ("Of the Characters of Women"). Even Dulness, in *The Dunciad*, is an unwed or parthenogenetic mother. Yet Pope produced no episode of admirable and fulfilled passion.

Two of his most polished works deal sympathetically with women penalized for subversive lust. In *Eloisa to Abelard* the lover has been castrated and the mistress consigned to a nunnery. In the *Elegy . . . to an Unfortunate Lady* a noble heiress has stabbed herself after eloping to a foreign country with a lover whom her guardian uncle had rejected. In both these poems the author encourages us to pity the lawbreaker: "Is it, in heav'n a crime to love too well?" he asks.

In *An Epistle to a Lady* the poet compliments his spinster friend Martha Blount (whom he briefly endows with a mythical husband and daughter) by opposing her to a series of corrupt, passionate mistresses or wives. In *The Rape of the Lock* the male figures are ridiculed and defeated, while the females remain unsatisfied.

Against this pattern it seems significant that the scenes of grotesque fantasy depend on images of unpleasant confusion and procreation. I am thinking of the Cave of Spleen in *The Rape of the Lock*, the Cave of Poverty and Poetry in Book One of *The Dunciad*, the bowers of the mud nymphs in Book Two of *The Dunciad*, and similar material.

Spleen of course means melancholy; and in the seventeenth century, it was commonplace to regard melancholy as the "balm of wit" and the "breath of poetry." When the gnome Umbriel descends to the Cave of Spleen, he is visiting a spring of creative imagination. Here Spleen herself is a goddess who can inspire the "poetic fit." Although the details of this allegorical cave are traditional, Pope colors them with phallic and erotic lights, with hints of perverse coition and gestation. So we get a linking of creativity with displaced sexuality and pain:

> Men prove with child, as pow'rful fancy works,
> And maids turn'd bottles, call aloud for corks.
> (*Rape of the Lock* IV, 53–54)

In Book Three of *The Dunciad* we meet the laureate Cibber lying with his head in the lap of the goddess Dulness while a dark, soporific dew falls and "raptures" overflow (lines 1–5)—a titillating scene. Two-thirds of the way through Book Three, another genius of false imagination appears—John Rich, producer of pantomimes. Here Pope brings in imagery of miraculous transformations of the universe echoing the representation of Christ in *The Messiah* and suggesting genesis and doomsday at once (lines 229–36). The chaos reaches its climax with an egg from which the human race is hatched. Again the work of creative imagination carries hints of asexual conception or parthenogenesis.

We have to notice how often Pope connected the act of composition with discomfort, muddle, misshapen birth and growth, delusive transformation. We do not meet order, dignity, and reality, but chaos, monsterhood, and illusion: "the chaos dark and deep, / Where nameless somethings in their causes sleep" (*Dunciad* I, 55–56, 59, 93–94). Attacking the decline of humanistic education, Pope deplores the standard practice of training schoolboys to compose Latin verses: "We hang one jingling padlock on the mind: / A poet the first day, he dips his quill; / And what the last? a very poet still" (*Dunciad* IV, 163–64).

These examples of disrespect for his vocation are from the last years of Pope's career and refer to bad poetry, not good. In his early work we read similar lines:

> Still run on poets in a raging vein,
> Ev'n to the dregs and squeezings of the brain;
> Strain out the last, dull droppings of their sense,
> And rhyme with all the rage of impotence.
>   (*Essay on Criticism*, lines 606–9)

This linking of composition to a hard stool and a limp penis also belongs to an attack on bad writing. But the images have too much power to rest in the boundaries prescribed by explicit meaning. When he refers directly to his own career as an author, Pope says, "I've had my purgatory here betimes, / And paid for all my satires, all my rhymes" (*Donne* IV, 5–6). It was only half-jokingly that he once said of the poet's calling, "Must one not be prepared to endure the reproaches of men, want and much fasting, nay martyrdom in its cause" (*Correspondence*, II, 227). The pleasure of creation loses itself in the toil and humiliation.

If one puts aside the link with authorship and considers unsublimated sexuality, the material points one along a more direct road but not to marriage, parenthood, and stability. The poet offers conventional denunciations of vice. But he also provides vivid descriptions of frustrated passion, titillating coquetry, tenderness outside marriage, and misery born in wedlock. The frailty and quick alterations of carnal appetite strike him more than its fruitfulness. He conveys a deep sympathy with the voluptuous impulse and deep uncertainty as to its consequence.

In *The Rape of the Lock*, disorderly lust glances at us from the first couplet; and it pounds on us in the final canto. "Die" for sexual climax, "thing" for vagina, "hair" displaced from the groin to the head, all remind one that the proper study of nubile girls is men.

"What dire offence from am'rous causes springs, / What mighty contests rise from trivial things, / I sing," says Pope as he begins a story connecting love with theft and war. The couplet sounds plain enough until we hear an echo of Horace joining the same themes and calling the vagina (or lust) a most shameful cause of war (*cunnus taeterrima belli / causa*—*Satires* I, iii,

107). Once we remember that Pope would translate "cunnus" as "thing," the language of decorum becomes a screen for impropriety.

In Canto Five of *The Rape of the Lock*, the battle of the sexes takes a more liberal form; and when Belinda defeats the Baron with a pinch of snuff, he says,

> Thou by some other shalt be laid as low.
> Nor think, to die dejects my lofty mind;
> All that I dread, is leaving you behind!
>
> (lines 98–100)

Here the poet openly, if indelicately, sympathizes with the natural impulse of young blood. So also in the early cantos of *The Rape of the Lock*, Pope celebrates the delight of Belinda in her own sexually provocative beauty:

> Now awful beauty puts on all its arms;
> The fair each moment rises in her charms,
> Repairs her smile, awakens ev'ry grace,
> And calls forth all the wonders of her face.
>
> (I, 139–42)

So also the sylphs—spirits whose job it is to guard Belinda's defensive and offensive weapons—are represented with wholehearted (though smiling) approval. Their humble work is to "tend the fair"; so long as the heroine refrains from matrimony, they strive to protect the arsenal of her beauty—

> To save the powder from too rude a gale,
> Nor let th'imprison'd essences exhale,
> To draw fresh colours from the vernal flow'rs,
> To steal from rainbows ere they drop in show'rs
> A brighter wash; to curl their waving hairs,
> Assist their blushes, and inspire their airs;
> Nay oft, in dreams, inventions we bestow,
> To change a *flounce*, or add a *furbelo*.
>
> (II, 93–100)

Belinda makes us live among changing appearances, unfixed emotions, fascinating discords, elegant but furious rivalries, stylized and comic wars. There is nothing placid, domestic, or parental about *The Rape of the Lock*. Its few snatches of security only prepare us for long passages of delightful un-easiness.

Yet in some masterful lines of elevated reasoning, one of Belinda's friends, named Clarissa, warns her of the transience of voluptuous pleasure and belligerent beauty. She reminds us that courtship ought to fix its goal in stable domesticity, marriage and motherhood:

> Since painted, or not painted, all shall fade,
> And she who scorns a man must die a maid;
> What then remains, but well our pow'r to use,
> And keep good humour still whate'er we lose.
>
> (V, 27–30)

This is sane as well as eloquent. Only, as it happens, when the Baron wished to snip off a lock of Belinda's hair, it was the same Clarissa who gave him the scissors.

In *The Rape of the Lock* the poet's obsession with time and change heightens a brief joy in youthful ardor. But ulti-mately it implies that creative imagination alone can triumph over age and death. The familiar theme of *monumentum aere perennius* brings together the sexual aspect of authorship and the lure of misdirected passion. Elsewhere Pope belittled the theme. Here, by invoking it ironically to close a battle of the sexes, he momentarily resolves his own doubts.

So at the end of the poem, yet once more reviving the ex-hausted pun on "die," once more identifying the eye of beauty with the eye of heaven, Pope brings nature and art together as he immortalizes the maiden whom he cannot enjoy. Here we meet that ideal of the poet as artist which enabled Pope to tran-scend his private self-disgust and his public role as guardian of the nation's morals.

> For, after all the murders of your eye,
> When, after millions slain, your self shall die;
> When those fair suns shall set, as set they must,
> And all those tresses shall be laid in dust;
> *This lock*, the muse shall consecrate to fame,
> And mid'st the stars inscribe *Belinda*'s name.
>
> (V, 145–50)

Years later, Pope took up the burden of sexuality with rather less of an effort to sound decorous. This was in *Sober Advice from Horace*, published anonymously in 1734. Here, however, the theme of lust itself becomes part of a political argument; and one should meet that argument before going on to the poem. To Pope, the most challenging aspect of implicit meaning presented itself in his criticism of the highest levels of English vice. From about the time he was forty, and continuing about fifteen years, the poet's judgment of his nation deepened in severity, and he invented subtler, yet keener, ways to reveal it.

The port of embarkation for these expeditions into outrage is unusually apparent in *An Essay on Man*. Here, in the third epistle, the poet displays a vision of the primitive condition of human society. This vision embraces a harmony between various realms of morality and value: private duty and public responsibility, virtue and power, the order of social privilege and the order of natural talent. In the *Essay* Pope represents humanity in the state of nature as embodying the ideal harmony. Kingship, virtue, piety, and wisdom stand united:

> 'Till then, by Nature crown'd, each Patriarch sate,
> King, priest, and parent of his growing state;
> On him, their second Providence, they hung,
> Their law his eye, their oracle his tongue.
> He from the wond'ring furrow call'd the food,
> Taught to command the fire, controul the flood,
> Draw forth the monsters of th'abyss profound,
> Or fetch th'aerial eagle to the ground.
>
> . . . .
>
> *Love* all the faith, and all th'allegiance then;
> For Nature knew no right divine in Men,
> No ill could fear in God; and understood
> A sov'reign being but a sov'reign good.[1]

It was from the contemplation of this empyrean that Pope came to judge the rich and the great. What he found of course

---

1. *Essay on Man* III, 215-22, 235-40. The last four lines quoted allude bitterly to the court's easy control over Parliament at the time when the poem was published (May, 1733).

was that the English social order rarely disclosed the correspondences he admired. The directors of the nation set more examples of vice than of virtue. The wealthy class largely overlapped with the frivolous class. The circle of talent bowed to the circle of corruption. Spokesmen for the houses of learning were vain and pedantic; at the head of religious institutions stood worldly, ambitious prelates.

To express his anger or disappointment, Pope used a categorical rhetoric that suited his poetic style. He juxtaposed group to group, example to class, ideal to reality. When he condemned, he described the evil as typical. When he praised, he handled the subject as a rare brightness in a world of shadows.

Pope's methods of satirical implication, therefore, gain strength from the contrast the poet habitually makes between style—including rhetorical forms—and meaning. As a satirist he gave extraordinary attention not only to nuances of implication but to the patterns of sound and rhythm in which he embodied them. These elements he fitted inside the parallels and antitheses of phrase or clause and the analogies or contrasts that shaped his paragraphs. His figures of speech could be pointedly brief, or they could expand the length of a paragraph or even (as a reiterated motif) of a poem, deepening the categorical tendencies of the rhetoric and poetic. So also his arguments moved discursively from general to particular, from example to universal and back. One poem balanced or opposed another, as the first *Moral Essay* (*To Cobham*), on male psychology, balanced the second (*To a Lady*), on female.

On all these levels Pope's constant effort is to redefine, regroup, to undermine old congruities and establish or hint at new ones. In his explicit arguments Pope seldom tried to inculcate fresh doctrines, but relied on traditional wisdom, on commonly accepted moral principles, or formulae. Maynard Mack has demonstrated the fullness of the tradition behind the sentences of *An Essay on Man*. "Its materials," he says, "are painstakingly traditional."[2] Earl Wasserman and Miriam Leranbaum have shown how much the third and fourth *Moral Es-*

2. Introduction to *An Essay on Man*, in Pope, *Poems*, III (i), p. xlii.

says (*Bathurst* and *Burlington*) owed to Aristotle.[3] Thomas Maresca has argued persuasively that in the imitations of Horace, Pope leaned heavily on the uncontested principles of pagan and Christian ethics which commentators elicited from the text of the ancient poet.[4] Yet in the freshest way Pope's genius built sparkling, challenging designs out of these common properties.

The chief effect of style on meaning in Pope's satires of the 1730s and 1740s is to group persons and ideas in discomforting ways. Since the clusters assembled and disconnected are based on moral relationships, the outcome is a questioning of assumptions often put forward and widely credited. Among these Pope's special tendency is to cast into doubt the proper association of rank with merit, virtue, or even good manners. Again and again in his poems the author invokes a natural hierarchy of established families who benevolently control the landed wealth and the government of the country—recalling the harmonious vision of *An Essay on Man*. But he implies that the social and moral boundaries can no longer be congruent. They have broken down; a heterogeneous mob has replaced the ordered community; and it takes in

> Whate'er of mungril no one class admits,
> A wit with dunces, and a dunce with wits.
> (*Dunciad* IV, 89–90)

A simple example is Pope's imitation of Horace *Satires* I, ii (*Sober Advice from Horace*), to which I now return. The Latin poem is a jocular mock-sermon on the dangers of adultery committed with respectable women. Horace directs his satire against men who feel dissatisfied with the sexual opportunities afforded them by slaves, freedwomen, or courtesans, and who insist on pursuing matrons. The individuals whom Horace singles out for explicit reproach are all male. Though he opens by

3. Earl R. Wasserman, *Pope's "Epistle to Bathurst"* (Baltimore: Johns Hopkins Press, 1960), p. 37 et passim; Miriam Leranbaum, *Alexander Pope's "Opus Magnum"* (Oxford: Clarendon Press, 1977), pp. 111–12, 117, 121, 125–26.

4. Thomas E. Maresca, *Pope's Horatian Poems* (Columbus: Ohio State University Press, 1966).

illustrating the theme of excess with instances of prodigality and avarice, once he arrives at the matter of adultery, he focuses his poem on it. While Horace dealt with persons of consequence, he did not draw attention to their rank.

Pope gives roughly equal representation to both sexes but makes his most scandalous examples female. He draws attention to the rank of his characters and connects lust with gluttony and avarice. In a mock-apparatus Pope ridicules the scholarship of Richard Bentley (whose emendations he was nevertheless willing to adopt) and endows him with a prurient sensibility.

The reason for the difference between the two poets is that under the appearance of ridiculing adulterers, Pope is busy endowing the great of the land with the worst vices. He deals with a king's mistress (line 81), a prime minister's infidelities (line 88), the venereal disease of a duchess (line 95), the lust of an archbishop (line 44). Even Bentley, enlisted as annotator *malgré soi*, was himself master of a great college and a cultivator of the Whig ministry in power.

We observe that several of Horace's types of masculine vice turn feminine in Pope's lines. Tigellius the singer becomes Mrs. Oldfield the actress (line 4); Fufidius changes into Fufidia (line 18); Rufillus, Rufa (line 29); Maltinus, Jenny (line 33). In other words, the poet refuses to let the women appear passive, or to imply that only the males of the ruling class are corrupt. Horace had assumed that men were the instigators of vice, and women the persons seduced (though not always resisting). Pope implicitly breaks down the barrier between the sexes, suggesting that on the highest levels women become unnaturally aggressive. To those readers who compared the imitation with the Latin original, Pope would have implied that English ladies of fashion differed from ancient Roman matrons in starting rather than responding to acts of lust. In a sense, this poem leads into Pope's second *Moral Essay, To a Lady*.

Far more broadly, Pope suggests that corruption makes strange bedfellows; and that vice brings together groups that ought to be kept apart. Where Horace blames a few men for disgracing their ancestors, Pope hints that the natural hierarchy which underpins civilized society has yielded to moral chaos. This is also what the effects of style and structure suggest. In his opening lines, the poet uses rhythm and sound patterns to clarify the irony of his tone:

> The Tribe of Templars, Play'rs, Apothecaries,
> Pimps, Poets, Wits, Lord Fanny's, Lady Mary's. . . .

The catalogue of lawyers, poets, etc., makes the kind of set one might expect to gather in a theater district that lies near the inns of court. But high-placed lords and ladies should have no close ties with actors, pimps, and the healers of venereal disease. Pope marks off "Lord Fanny's, Lady Mary's" with a caesura but places them at the climax of his catalogue. In rhythm and sound patterns they are unlike the earlier series but tied to it. Yet they are, in sound, curiously like each other. Thus Pope implies the ambiguous sexuality of Hervey—the couplet has feminine endings—and the scandalous association of both him and Lady Mary with dubious characters.

Two aspects of the language of the poem add to such effects. Where Horace uses plain words like *inguina, cunnus,* and *muto* (all mistranslated in the Loeb edition), Pope enlists either a suggestive euphemism like *part* (line 87) or a pun like *frigate* (line 62). The consequent dazzle of ambiguities (*rise,* line 88; *stiff,* line 152; above all, *thing,* passim) enriches the suggestion of barriers breaking down. Maynard Mack has pointed out an exquisite instance. When Pope writes,

> Suppose that honest part that rules us all,
> Should rise, and say—"Sir Robert! or Sir Paul!"
> (lines 87–88)

the reference to a prime minister and a statesman evokes question time in the House of Commons; "part" suggests a genital "member," and therefore Member of Parliament; and so a fornicating phallus invades the high process of legislation.[5] Another pair of realms that should be kept apart, merge.

The categories that fascinated Pope, in the satires, were

5. See Mack, *The Garden and the City* (Toronto: University of Toronto Press, 1969), p. 166.

those of public and private, high rank and low. Against these he pitted other categories like good and bad, tasteful and vulgar. Often his rhetoric moves from the personal and private world to that of public responsibility, or from the latter to the former. Invariably, he assumes that a harmony between these worlds is natural.

Such modulations depend on Pope's starting from familiar doctrines (what I should call formulae) and identifiable examples. As a moralist, he may state his doctrine in a paradox, but the teaching itself is likely to be conventional, not difficult and not too subtle. Pope still has a tendency of his own which differentiates him from the usual preacher of Christian doctrine and from most satirists. In searching for models of virtue, he looks instinctively to actors who are offstage—of middle rank or out of favor. If he must have virtuous kings, statesmen, or bishops, he likes to secure ancients, foreigners, or Englishmen long dead.

By these means Pope can imply harsh judgments on the most powerful figures of his own age without endangering himself. The judgment grows more severe, and the class of corrupt persons more extensive, until we arrive at the *Epilogue to the Satires, 1740,* and the last book of *The Dunciad.* Finally, as in *The Dunciad* (Book IV), Pope was willing to blacken the character of whole orders of humanity. Earlier, he tried to appear selective; for his selectiveness was carefully weighted. Thus in picking names to celebrate, the poet did not always avoid men of rank. Among the subjects of his eulogies are Bathurst, Cobham, Oxford (father and son), and Bolingbroke. But he picked his noble heroes from the files of Jacobites, Tories, and opposition Whigs. Otherwise, he favored commoners of middle rank, like Kyrle,[6] Martha Blount,[7] and Dr. Arbuthnot.

Pope usually mentioned bishops only in order to blame them.[8] But when he wished to display his impartiality and

6. *Moral Essays* III (*To Bathurst*), lines 249–90.
7. *Moral Essays* II (*To a Lady*), lines 249–92.
8. For contemptuous or ambiguous allusions to bishops in general or particular, see the following: *Moral Essays* I (*To Cobham*), lines 88–90;

bestow compliments on them, he named four, starting with one indeed close to the court but ending climactically with Berkeley, who had been sponsored by the Tory Swift, had been chaplain to the Jacobite Duke of Wharton, and had gained his elevation in spite of his connections:

> Ev'n in a Bishop I can spy Desert;
> Secker is decent, Rundel has a heart,
> Manners with Candour are to Benson giv'n,
> To Berkeley, ev'ry Virtue under Heav'n.
> (*Epilogue to the Satires* II, 70–73)

Only the tribute to Berkeley is unequivocal. If we collect all the epithets, the poet drives us into separating the order of bishops from the moral order of decency, charity, candor, and virtue in general. "Ev'n" and "spy" suggest a minute search for the few exceptions to the rule. Berkeley has a strong place in his line, emphasized by the caesura and enriched by the echo of his name's sound and rhythm in "virtue" (*vartue*). Though he ends the series, he makes a contrast to the preceding trio, two of whom divide a line and the third occupies a weak place in a slow line of bathetic compliment.

So also if Pope did praise a very rich government official in Ralph Allen, he went out of his way to call him "low-born";[9] and as Erskine-Hill says, Allen's career rested on genuine service to the nation and was independent of Walpole or party.[10] Although I dwell on the subtle or indirect conveyance of meaning, Pope could be perfectly open at the same time. His gift for innuendo did not keep him from declaring explicitly what he was busy implying:

> But does the Court a worthy Man remove?
> That instant, I declare, he has my Love:
> I shun his Zenith, court his mild Decline. . . .
> (*Epilogue to the Satires* II, 74–76)

Horace *Satires* II, i, 152; Horace *Satires* I, ii, 39–44; *Epistle to Arbuthnot*, line 100; *Epilogue to the Satires* I, 132, 146, and II, 33, 70–74; *Dunciad* I, 28; IV, 593.

9. Original reading of *Epilogue to the Satires* I, 135.

10. *Social Milieu of Alexander Pope* (New Haven: Yale University Press, 1975), p. 237.

Pope's distaste for kings and conquerors is too obvious to need mention. Recently even his respect for the Emperor Augustus as an admirable alternative to the degenerate Georges has been persuasively doubted by meticulous scholars.[11] Miriam Leranbaum pointed out the large number of "great" men alluded to in the first *Moral Essay* (*To Cobham*): "The emphasis is upon rulers, kings, statesmen—exalted figures of all kinds."[12] She observed further that the matching poem, *To a Lady*, also abounds in high personages, and that for part of the poem Pope uses "queen" as a synonym for "woman."[13] Leranbaum connected these poems with the fourth epistle of *An Essay on Man*, which again has a good many allusions to kings in general and to certain rulers and tyrants in particular: Alexander, Caesar, Titus, Marcus Aurelius, Charles XII of Sweden—of whom two are treated as admirable (Titus and Marcus Aurelius) and the others as baneful. The same epistle of *An Essay on Man* opens and closes with a panegyric of Bolingbroke, and the first epistle opens with an apostrophe to him. In all three places he is opposed to kings. Bolingbroke was of course the intellectual leader of the opposition to Walpole's government and to George II's court.

We may infer that the most exciting subject for Pope's ridicule was George II. An analysis of the methods applied to his majesty's character will bring out Pope's methods in general. The operations begin at the level of common nouns. In poems published during the dozen years beginning in 1731, the word "king" constantly appears to point the generalizations about human nature and morality. But somehow the poet uses the name seldom with respect and often with contempt: "the pride of kings," "a lunatic king," "public spirit its great cure a crown."[14] A couplet like that in the fourth epistle of *An Essay on Man* gives the direction of Pope's pressure on the word:

11. Howard Weinbrot, "History, Horace, and Augustus Caesar," *Eighteenth-Century Studies* 7 (1974): 391–414; Malcolm Kelsall, "Augustus and Pope," *Huntington Library Quarterly* 39 (1976): 117–31.

12. *Alexander Pope's "Opus Magnum,"* p. 72.

13. Ibid., p. 74.

14. *Essay on Man* I, 2; II, 268; IV, 172.

> Stuck o'er with titles and hung round with strings,
> That thou may'st be by kings, or whores of kings. . . .
>
> (lines, 205–6)

In the *Epistle to Burlington* the poet foresees that some future king will follow the example of the earl, whose ideas are "worthy kings" (lines 195, 204). The notion of the future implicitly excludes the present; and if the projects are suitable for kings, it strikes us that the monarch in power has not seen fit to carry them out. We might infer therefore that kingship as such is a concept excluding George II.

In the *Epistle to Bathurst* the word "king" appears only in connection with avarice (lines 72, 78, 401). The poet suggests that bribes are welcomed by a king and may determine royal policy. In his imitation of Horace *Satires* II, i, Pope uses the word "king" only once and then ambiguously, to say that he himself writes sober, moral poems such as a king might read (line 152). The remark exudes irony because near the beginning of his poem Pope says that George II does not read poetry (line 35). A few weeks later, in the second epistle of *An Essay on Man* (published in February, 1733), "kings" are an instance of presumption (line 244), and "king" is what a lunatic thinks himself to be (line 268).

If we now skip to the last epistle of *An Essay on Man*, we see the process speed up, and discover a concentration of "king's" used with offputting connotations: fools fight for kings, wish to be kings, are ennobled by kings, become the favorites of kings.[15] The poet draws a contrast between the immortal fame of his hero Bolingbroke and the shortlived reputation of kings (IV, 387). The process does not pause here but goes on to the last book of *The Dunciad*, where Pope lets himself ridicule the "*Right Divine* of kings to govern wrong" (line 188).

When the poet's text failed him, as being too exposed, he could seek refuge in his mock-commentary. In this sanctuary (like Swift in the notes to the fifth edition of *A Tale of a Tub*) he could conjure up not one but two editors quarreling with one another over the meaning of a line, and by this device could

15. Ibid., IV, 157, 160, 206, 289.

produce with safety insinuations against George II. In *The Dunciad* (IV, 181–82) there is a commentators' quibble over a supposed allusion to verses by Claudian that describe liberty as flourishing under a good king. In the course of the disagreement, "Scriblerus" observes that liberty is often confused with monarchy; but "Bentley" retorts that "Liberty was never *lost*, or *went away* with so good a grace, as under a good king"!

In *An Epistle to a Lady* ("Of the Characters of Women") the use of "queen" suffers a similar deformation. Here, in a gallery of female portraits, the only picture of a queen is a flatterer's deception (lines 181–86). Pope declares that women generally want power and pleasure: every lady would be queen for life (line 218). Thus he makes the word itself into a term of abuse for vicious, megalomaniac females; and we hear the contemptuous phrase, "a whole sex of queens" (line 219).

As a common noun, of course, "king" easily alternates with its near synonyms. "Tyrant" and "prince" appear alongside it. But all these are mingled with the proper names of various rulers, from Alexander the Great to George II—or with allusions plainly identifying them. Except for Titus and Marcus Aurelius, the names receive ambiguous or sinister overtones. In the *Epistle to Cobham* (lines 146–53)—published during the same month as the last epistle of *An Essay on Man*—Pope has a passage assembling an ugly gang of individual rulers, as if to balance the use of the common noun in the *Essay*. Although explicitly chosen to illustrate the inconsistency of human nature, almost every one is dispraised in an epithet: buffoon, perjur'd, godless, bigot, faithless, duped, fool.[16]

This example hardly misleads one. Pope's satires do provide momentary glimpses of a king's behaving himself decently, but such acts tend to appear out of character for the particular monarch; and in representing them, the poet seems to want a contrast to the inactivity of George II. Thus Pope describes Charles II, James II, and Louis XIV as tolerating satirical poetry. But he

16. Caesar, Otho, Louis XIV; Charles V, Philip II, and Philip V of Spain; Cromwell, Victor Amadeus II of Sardinia, and the Duke of Orleans (Regent of France).

does so in response to a friend who warns him against enraging the present powers;[17] and he treats the phenomenon as contrary to what one might expect of each king. The greatest concentration of admirable royal gestures, in the *Epistle to Augustus*, invites us to set the heroism or patronage of half a dozen kings against the lack of those qualities in King George.[18] And yet several of these examples are themselves ambiguous: Charles I pensioned Quarles (line 387); Charles II "debauch'd" the muses (line 152); William III knighted Blackmore (line 387).

In the late poems generally, miscellaneous rulers are named to be censured or ridiculed. Pope gives special attention to wicked or stupid figures: kings, usurpers, and emperors whom the poet might freely identify, yet who, by association with the class of kings, would stain the mantle of George II. By admitting his exceptions, the poet strengthens the innuendo against the type.

As early as the *Epistle to Burlington* (published in December, 1731), Pope contrasts the good taste of his lordship with the doubtful taste of Louis XIV and Nero (lines 71–72). In *An Essay on Man*, Epistle IV, along with the common noun, the poet sneers at Caesar three times, as well as Alexander the Great and Charles XII of Sweden.[19] Alexander and Caesar had already been stigmatized in Epistle I as natural disasters (lines 159–60). Midas, in the *Epistle to Arbuthnot*, is cursed by Apollo with the ears of an ass (lines 69–82).

As one reads through the poems, it becomes clear that Pope intends us to refer back and forth among them in order to perfect identifications which are hinted at in separate places. Lord Fanny, Sporus, and Narcissus are thus united.[20] So also the names for Lady Mary Wortley Montagu and her husband. She alone may be Fufidia, Sappho, or simply Lady Mary,[21] which

17. Horace *Satires* II, i, 111–14.
18. Horace *Epistles* II, i, 7, 8, 140–42, 375, 380–83.
19. Lines 146, 220, 244.
20. Horace *Satires* II, i, 6; II, ii, 101; *Epistle to Arbuthnot*, lines 149, 305–33; *Dunciad* IV, 103.
21. Horace *Satires* I, ii, 18, and II, i, 83; *Moral Essays* II, 24; *Epistle to Arbuthnot*, line 101; Horace *Satires* I, ii, 2; Horace *Epistles* I, i, 164.

is to say, lustful, unclean, avaricious, and bluestocking. (Sir Edward and she together are Gripus, Shylock, or Avidien and his wife—all usurers.)[22] So when readers are not linking the ambiguous sexuality of Hervey to the florid style of his prose, they may be blending the stinginess ascribed to Lady Mary with her alleged carnality. Alternatively, they may assure themselves that various names allude to the same person because they notice a cluster of traits circulating unchanged. The style of wit and the courtly prominence of Sporus in the *Epistle to Arbuthnot* persuade us that Hervey is the reference of "H——vy" in the *Epilogue to the Satires*.[23]

Even so with Caesar: Pope openly alluded to George II as "Caesar" in an imitation of Horace.[24] A year later, in the last epistle of *An Essay on Man*, he mentioned "Caesar with a senate at his heels," and juxtaposed him to Marcellus in exile—thus inviting us to set George II against Bolingbroke.[25] At the very same time, when he refers to Caesar retreating from Britain and risking his empire for a punk, we may perhaps think of the king leaving England to join Madame Walmoden in Hanover.[26]

Alternatively, Pope may suppress the word "king" and bring together traits well known as marks of his majesty: bearishness, the habit of kicking when angry, the domination of the royal mind (such as it was) by Queen Caroline, the prime minister's power over his master. " 'Tis a bear's talent not to kick, but hug," may be an allusion to George II.[27] The following lines (gathering in six of the seven cardinal sins!) certainly are such an allusion:

> Know, there are Rhymes, which (fresh and fresh apply'd)
> Will cure the arrant'st Puppy of his Pride.
> Be furious, envious, slothful, mad or drunk,
> Slave to a Wife or Vassal to a Punk,

22. *Essay on Man* IV, 280; Horace *Satires* II, i, 103, and II, ii, 49.
23. *Epilogue to the Satires* I, 72.
24. Horace *Satires* I, ii, 21.
25. *Essay on Man* IV, 257-58.
26. *Moral Essays* I (*To Cobham*), 81-84.
27. Horace *Satires* II, i, 87.

A Switz, a High-dutch, or a Low-dutch Bear—
All that we ask is but a patient Ear.[28]

One of Pope's most mischievous devices is to insult George and Caroline by reviling their flatterers. The obvious example occurs in the earliest imitation of Horace. Here, Pope's friend Fortescue advises the poet to write something in praise of the king. Pope replies with some lines of parody of what Blackmore, Budgell, and Cibber have written in praise of William III and George II. Fortescue suggests that he praise the queen and the royal children. The poet replies that the ears of majesty are too "nice" to bear his verses. But the satire on bad poets irresistibly attaches itself to the royal persons; and in a closing ambiguity, Pope deliciously evokes his monarch's indifference to literature of all sorts:

And justly *Caesar* scorns the Poet's Lays,
It is to *History* he trusts for praise.[29]

Queen Caroline undergoes a similar blackwash in the second *Moral Essay* (*To a Lady*), when Pope ostensibly despairs of finding an honest portrait of her, because flattering authors and artists adorn her always and mechanically with conventional virtues:

One certain Portrait may (I grant) be seen,
Which Heav'n has varnish'd out, and made a *Queen*:
The same for ever! and describ'd by all
With Truth and Goodness, as with Crown and Ball:
Poets heap Virtues, Painters Gems at will,
And show their zeal, and hide their want of skill.
(lines 181–86)

The innuendo is of course that the artists must manufacture the virtues because Caroline has none of them.

This device can be pointed, as when, in the *Epilogue to the Satires*, the poet denounces those who "make saints of

28. Horace *Epistles* I, i, 58–64. For the seventh sin, see line 56. For detailed evidence, see Mack, *The Garden and the City*, pp. 128–41.
29. Horace *Satires* II, i, 35–36.

queens, and gods of kings" (II, 225). But it can easily be generalized to apply to other persons of consequence; and in one of the most dazzling passages of his poetry, Pope brings in bishops, judges, and statesmen. This is the first *Moral Essay*, *To Cobham*. Here, in a justly famous paragraph, Pope argues that most poets (or artists) turn, for their examples of virtue, to the upper levels of society. He then transforms the fact into satire by recommending the practice. Actually, he says, it is so hard to be virtuous in a great position that whoever succeeds in doing so deserves unusual praise:

> 'Tis from high Life high Characters are drawn;
> A Saint in Crape is twice a Saint in Lawn;
> A Judge is just, a Chanc'lor juster still;
> A Gownman, learn'd; a Bishop, what you will;
> Wise, if a Minister; but, if a King,
> More wise, more learn'd, more just, more ev'ry thing.
> Court-virtues bear, like Gems, the highest rate,
> Born where Heav'n's influence scarce can penetrate:
> In life's low vale, the soil the virtues like,
> They please as Beauties, here as Wonders strike.
>
> (lines 87–96)

The method of implication derives again from the way the technique of verse divides and unites categories: lower clergy and episcopacy are separated instead of being united as the church; so also are a lower justice and the chancellor, who ought to be collected in the law. "Saint in crape" and "saint in lawn" are parallel in form and rhythm. Yet the parson might be a saint while the bishop could only gain promotion through corruption. "Judge-just," as alliteration, balances "chanc'lor-juster," with its repeated endings and sibilants. But the judge is far likelier than the chancellor is to keep his integrity. The categories of true and specious goodness are thus closely joined precisely as they are set apart. "Crape" opposes "lawn" in sound as "judge" opposes "chanc'lor." In the paragraph as a whole the ideas of high and low are similarly split and rejoined.

Such operations bring the whole relation of example to postulate into doubt. Pope can illustrate an aphorism with an instance that weakens it, as when he says that poets want only to enjoy their garden and book "in quiet," and then praises Swift for saving "the rights a court attack'd."[30] More abstractly, he even challenges the distinction between reality and fiction. Thus Pope offers us historical examples, identified by name or otherwise, along with veiled pseudonyms which can be penetrated by a giveaway trait or association, and, as well, with utterly imaginary examples which discourage speculation. Sometimes he combines these various procedures, by using the real name harmlessly and then following it at once with a pseudonym and satiric characterization of the same person: the Addison-Atticus passage in the *Epistle to Arbuthnot* is a cunning example (lines 192–214). At his boldest, in dealing with the king, Pope can use the very name of George, but so ambiguously that one reader might think the reference innocuous (or complimentary) while another could see it as an insult:

> I sought no homage from the Race that write;
> I kept, like Asian Monarchs, from their sight:
> Poems I heeded (now be-rym'd so long)
> No more than Thou, great *George!* a Birth-day Song.
> (*Epistle to Arbuthnot*, lines 220–23)

(That is, the king is so indifferent to poetry that he cannot notice it even when it is in praise of himself.) The magnificent climax of this technique is of course the opening and closing lines of the *Epistle to Augustus* (Horace *Epistles* II, i, 1–30, 390–419). Both these passages may be read as either eulogy or vituperation.

If we consider the entire range of such innuendoes and the classes of men and ideas to which they are applied, we may say that ultimately, Pope establishes two realms of implication in his satires—one, conventionally didactic; the other, boldly subversive. One shares the orientation of the explicit meaning and develops it in the usual way by imagery, analogy, irony, etc. The other has a different center, different coordinates, from the explicit meaning, which it employs as a code or a screen.

30. Horace *Epistles* II, i (*To Augustus*), 198–99, 221–24.

Maynard Mack calls the one thematic and the other topical.[31]

Thus although I have made much of the subversive implications of the first *Moral Essay* (*To Cobham*), that poem has a familiar orientation as well, implicitly supported by Pope's choice of images. This design starts from the explicit question whether or not one can secure a true knowledge of the inner characters of men.

Pope offers two points of view, the scepticism of Montaigne and the effort made by Locke to establish an area of demonstrable knowledge. Pope claims that he can arrive at true knowledge by way of the concept of a ruling passion. But for two-thirds of the poem he illustrates the sceptical position.

The imagery of the epistle to Cobham opposes effects of light to elements drawn from external nature: landscape, plants, animals. Pope implies that light and color are more deceptive than line and shape. He implicitly links human deceitfulness with the ancient principle that line is more reliable than color. He associates virtue with things that grow naturally, vice with things that blaze.

On this level the poem is not dangerous but quite satisfactory, with the images implicitly bearing out the argument. It is when we shift our attention from the pattern of images to the choice of human examples that the subversive implications rise to trouble us.

The same analysis applies to the last epistle of *An Essay on Man*. Here the poet discusses the best ways for men to achieve happiness, and says that "fled from monarchs, St. John, [it] dwells with thee" (line 18). Conventionally, this verse alludes to expressions like "happy as a king," and implies that kings are not in fact happy. But subversively, it implies that the corruption of George II is less likely to produce happiness than the integrity of his opponent, Bolingbroke.

So also, expounding the principle that God works in orderly ways and does not often suspend the rules governing the universe, Pope observes that adherence to order may sometimes subject virtuous persons to illness and pain:

31. *The Garden and the City*, p. 163.

Think we, like some weak prince, th'Eternal Cause
Prone for his fav'rites to reverse his laws?

(lines 121–22)

Conventionally, here, Pope is implying that divine justice is the model for earthly justice. But subversively, he implies that under George II, royal mistresses and favored courtiers may commit crimes with impunity.

One of the strongest examples of what I may call the bipolarity of Pope's implications is a passage in the *Epilogue to the Satires*. It illustrates his fascination with the connection between private and public realms. Pope starts from the assumption that domestic virtue has a direct relation to public performance, that a faithless husband cannot be an honest statesman. He then proceeds to dissolve the line between the realms, and blame a corrupt politician as if his infidelities sprang from the same cause as his misgovernment. The well-known lines about Vice owned by Greatness make the process splendidly visible:

> *Vice* is undone, if she forgets her Birth,
> And stoops from Angels to the Dregs of Earth:
> But 'tis the *Fall* degrades her to a Whore;
> Let *Greatness* own her, and she's mean no more:
> Her birth, her Beauty, Crowds and Courts confess,
> Chaste Matrons praise her, and grave Bishops bless:
> In golden Chains the willing World she draws,
> And hers the Gospel is, and hers the Laws. . . .
>
> (*Epilogue* I, 141–48)

The explicit meaning is deepened by the association of vice with the Scarlet Whore; and as James Osborn has shown, the particular scarlet whore intended was the Empress Theodora. Yet, as Osborn has also shown, there was a hidden, far more scandalous allusion, in these lines, to the marriage of Walpole with his mistress Maria Skerrett; and the description of Vice represents her triumph.[32]

The poem does not call upon us to choose between these implications. Conventionally, Pope associates the career of vice

32. James M. Osborn, "Pope, the Byzantine Empress, and Walpole's Whore," *Review of English Studies*, n.s., 6 (1955): 372–82.

with the fall of angels and the rise of the Whore. Subversively, he ties it to the marriage of Molly Skerrett. Neither implication excludes the other, but the two move in different directions. The failure to accept such bipolarity has led some scholars to disregard the topical meaning for the thematic or the latter for the former, whereas the poet usually is playing with both at once, and letting the second peep out from behind the first.[33]

I think we can apply a similar analysis to Pope's concept of heroism. Scholars have noticed his habit of setting up the moral and social values traditionally belonging to the country house as vastly superior to those traditionally assigned to a royal court.[34] This opposition blends with an old political tradition of a country party, based in the gentry, which resisted the measures of the court. When the Tory-Whig alignments emerged in the late 1670s, they cut across the court-and-country alignments, which endured along with them. In poems that seem to place rural contentment before urban activity, Pope is often invoking as well the old political antithesis between country and court. Like Swift, he could distinguish unproductive stockbrokers or financiers from productive merchants or tradesmen. It is the former that he liked to merge with Walpole and the court. If Pope habitually embodied his own values in a cultivated, politically active country gentleman like Arthur Browne,[35] he also assumed that such a figure would for patriotic reasons resist the government in power. Here then is a concept of heroism in keeping with that of Dryden after the Revolution and of Swift after the death of Queen Anne.

In the late satires, however, Pope's bipolarity also shows itself in his treatment of this sort of hero. Ostensibly, he may place the uses of retirement before those of public office during

33. Cf. Barbara Lauren's quarrel with T. E. Maresca in her essay, "Pope's *Epistle to Bolingbroke*," *Studies in English Literature* 15 (1975): 419–30.

34. G. R. Hibbard, "The Country House Poem of the Seventeenth Century," *Journal of the Warburg and Courtauld Institutes* 19 (1956): 159–74; Mack, *The Garden and the City*, pp. 77–115; Erskine-Hill, *The Social Milieu of Alexander Pope*, pp. 279–317.

35. Horace *Epistles* II, ii.

a reign of corruption. The country gentleman may therefore appear to be a truly heroic figure, reminding us of Dryden's cousin John Driden. Yet as T. R. Edwards suggests, the poet as such can be recognized as Pope's hidden hero; and it is for this reason that, so early as *An Essay on Criticism*, we see the poet described as a warrior.[36] I find it significant that in this youthful, hopeful poem, Pope was willing to draw an analogy between writers and monarchs or conquerors:

> Like Kings we lose the Conquests gain'd before,
> By vain Ambition still to make them more. . . .
> (lines 64-65)

> A prudent Chief not always must display
> His Pow'rs in *equal Ranks*, and *fair Array*,
> But with th'*Occasion* and the *Place* comply,
> *Conceal* his Force, nay seem sometimes to *Fly*.[37]
> (lines 175-78)

In the pessimistic *Epistle to Augustus* the parallel becomes an antithesis:

> Yet let me show, a Poet's of some weight,
> And (tho' no Soldier) useful to the State. . . .
> I scarce can think him such a worthless thing,
> Unless he praise some monster of a King. . . .
> (lines 203-4, 209-10)

For now it is precisely as an independent gentleman that the poet is heroic. It is by resisting the blandishments of pensions and offices, by refusing to serve a corrupted crown, that the poet shows his virtue:

> I cannot like, Dread Sir! your Royal Cave;
> Because I see by all the Tracks about,
> Full many a Beast goes in, but none comes out.
> (Horace *Epistles* I, i, 115-17)

Thus on the one hand, Pope recommends and identifies himself with "chiefs, out of war, and statesmen, out of place."[38] He

---

36. *This Dark Estate* (Berkeley and Los Angeles: University of California Press, 1963), p. 16.

37. Cf. lines 508-14, 715-18.

38. Horace *Satires* II, i, 126.

celebrates Cobham as a gardener,[39] Bathurst "unspoil'd by wealth,"[40] and the Man of Ross making grandeur blush.[41] He implicitly praises himself for being the friend of men like Caryll and Bethel.

On the other hand, Pope exalts his own heroic character as bold moralist in verse, driving vice before him—"un-plac'd, unpension'd, no man's heir, or slave."[42] It is Pope in his own right who feels proud "to see / Men not afraid of God, afraid of me."[43] As the voice of heroic virtue, or even as "God's deputy" (in the words of T. R. Edwards),[44] he implicitly congratulates men like Burlington for being chosen among the poet's friends:

> Enough for half the Greatest of these days
> To 'scape my Censure, not expect my Praise:
> Are they not rich? what more can they pretend?
> Dare they to hope a Poet for their Friend?
> (*Epilogue to the Satires* II, 112–15)

Not only does he become the standard of merit; he records it. So Pope holds the authority that makes Hough and Digby immortal,[45] that damns Sporus and annihilates King George. In this ancient sense it is he who assigns the most splendid rewards for true greatness; honor derives from him as the fountain, and not from the king:[46]

> Sages and Chiefs long since had birth
>   E're Caesar was, or Newton nam'd,
> These rais'd new Empires o'er the Earth,
>   And Those new Heav'ns and Systems fram'd;
>
> Vain was the chief's and sage's pride
>   They had no Poet and they dyd!

39. *Moral Essays* I.
40. *Moral Essays* II, 226.
41. Ibid., line 281.
42. Horace *Satires* II, i, 116.
43. *Epilogue to the Satires* II, 208–9.
44. *This Dark Estate*, p. 92.
45. *Epilogue to the Satires* II, 240–41.
46. Cf. *Epilogue to the Satires* II, 234–47.

In vain they schem'd, in vain they bled
They had no Poet and are dead!
(Horace *Odes* IV, ix, 9–16)

From such a height it becomes feasible for the poet to connect the two poles of his ideal. By depicting himself as independent gentry, winning his power from being out of the great world, he implicitly brings both heroisms together:

Content with little, I can piddle here
On Broccoli and mutton, round the year;
But ancient friends, (tho' poor, or out of play)
That touch my Bell, I cannot turn away.
'Tis true, no Turbots dignify my boards,
But gudgeons, flounders, what my Thames affords.
To Hounslow-heath I point, and Bansted-down,
Thence comes your mutton, and these chicks my own:
From yon old wallnut-tree a show'r shall fall;
And grapes, long-lingring on my only wall,
And figs, from standard and espalier join:
The dev'l is in you if you cannot dine.
Then cheerful healths (your mistress shall have place)
And, what's more rare, a poet shall say *grace*.
(Horace *Satires* II, ii, 137–50)

In these genial lines, offering old-fashioned, rustic hospitality, the poet who can speak with the voice of God, who defies prelates, politicians, and tyrants—

Ye tinsel insects! whom a court maintains,
That counts your beauties only by your stains—
(*Epilogue to the Satires* II, 220–21)

wears his other mantle, that of an honest country gentleman.[47] Simultaneously, by cherishing the title of "poet" and echoing the language of Horace, he reminds us that it is his creative genius—the power that immortalized Belinda as well as Bolingbroke—which confers such authority upon Pope.

47. Mack, *The Garden and the City*, pp. 188–231.

CHAPTER IV

Austen: The Heroism of the Quotidian
❦

Austen's life belongs to the generation of Wordsworth and Coleridge. She deeply admired the poems of Cowper; those of Scott and Byron pleased her. Yet her mind and art clung to the habits of an earlier period stretching from Dryden to Johnson.

As an example of my principles, Austen deserves minute attention because she is hard to catch speaking out. Few authors conceal their opinions on subjects of controversy so well as Austen, screening her thoughts behind those of her characters. Anyone familiar with the novels of Scott knows how much Austen leaves out of her work. She hardly describes the physical appearance of her characters. In *Pride and Prejudice* we never learn the color of Elizabeth Bennet's eyes or of Darcy's hair. Austen does not expatiate on politics. In *Emma* we are not told what Mr. Knightley thinks of the Prince of Wales. Austen avoids religious debate and the particulars of Christian doctrine, though fifty percent of her heroes (and two of her fools) are clergymen. She gives no representation of sexual passion at its feverish height; yet her main characters include an illegitimate daughter (Harriet Smith, in *Emma*), the seducer of an orphan (Willoughby, in *Sense and Sensibility*), three runaway girls and their lovers (Kitty Bennet, in *Pride and Prejudice*; Maria and

Julia Bertram, in *Mansfield Park*), and an unctuous widow who elects to be the mistress of a double-dealing gentleman (Mrs. Clay, in *Persuasion*).[1]

Critics sometimes condemn Austen's omissions as faults. Sometimes they blame them on her ignorance of the subjects or her distaste for the themes. I wish to suggest another possibility, that the elements of her greatness require such omissions.

The mark of Austen's stories is the inwardness of the action—the novelist's preoccupation with self-knowledge. If one reflects on the history of narrative, including epic, drama, romance, and the novel, two features will distinguish Austen from the bulk of her predecessors. For them the problems to be studied were those of attracting and holding people one loves, of winning and keeping power or wealth, or else of destroying enemies. In this literature the protagonist normally was sure of his own desires but not of the motives of those around him. He often felt divided between opposing impulses, but he knew what the impulses really were. It was the darkness of other people's characters that troubled him; it was the obstacles they put in his way that complicated the action.

But for Austen the obstacles lie within, and the story is one of self-discovery. At the turning point of *Pride and Prejudice*, Elizabeth Bennet says, "Till this moment, I never knew myself" (p. 208). In *Emma* Mr. Knightley hovers until the heroine sees for herself (at long last) that she loves him. In *Persuasion*, Anne Elliot waits for Wentworth to stop misguiding himself and to realize that he cannot love anyone but her.

Mansfield Park is exceptional. Henry Crawford may lack self-knowledge; but Fanny Price fully understands her own devotion to Edmund Bertram. Yet as if to expiate this wisdom, she must keep it secret until Edmund wears out his illusions concerning Mary Crawford. The drama of the novel turns on Fanny's need to guard the single fact that dominates her character.

Elinor Dashwood, in *Sense and Sensibility*, knows herself

---

1. In *Mansfield Park* Mary Crawford leaves her uncle's house because he brings his mistress to live with him (p. 41).

and her lover perfectly well. The obstacles between them are indeed external, and the novel has the least adventurous design of all Austen's finished works. Even here we can discern an approach to the theme of self-knowledge, because the accomplishment of the action, apart from the various love affairs, is the discovery of Elinor's real nature by a sister and mother who had grossly undervalued her depth. It is when the two of them appreciate Elinor's complexity that they come to a proper judgment of their own character. One of the finest turns in the novel is the conversation in which Elinor undeceives her volatile sister about her own anguish over Edward Ferrars (pp. 262–64).

Of course, the novels abound in external actions. But a surprising number of these happen offstage with the reader only getting reports of them. So also Austen is exceptionally novelistic in representing most of the "onstage" incidents not directly but as impressions of one of her characters, especially the heroine. In *Sense and Sensibility*, Elinor's consciousness provides the main arena of the action. We learn that her beloved Edward has not married Lucy Steele, by watching her receive the information (p. 360). In *Persuasion* the novelist lets us see Louisa Musgrove's fall directly; but she passes the burden of what follows back and forth between herself and Anne Elliot.

This technique adds humor, pathos, or irony to incident after incident, and makes tiny gestures resonate with significance. It is also a brilliant method of endowing a modest protagonist with heroic stature. Merely because we see so much through her eyes, the heroine becomes the central, dominating figure. But the device also magnifies the inwardness of the plot.

If self-knowledge is the theme *par excellence* of Austen's work, it is not therefore detached from the ancient, ubiquitous subject of all forms of narrative, namely the darkness of other people's character. Elinor Dashwood puts this plainly when she says,

> I have frequently detected myself in . . . a total misapprehension of character in some point or other: fancying people so much more gay or grave, or ingenious or stupid than they really are, and I can hardly tell why, or in what the deception originated.

Sometimes one is guided by what they say of themselves, and very frequently by what other people say of them, without giving oneself time to deliberate and judge. (p. 93)

The correction of such misapprehensions belongs to the process of self-discovery, through which it makes the substance of the story. Thanks to such misapprehensions, inward and outward, Austen's villains trick themselves as much as they trick their victims. The old tradition of villainy involved deliberate hypocrisy. In Maskall (Congreve's Double Dealer) or in Blifil (Fielding's devilish prig), or again in Lovelace (Richardson's archschemer), the criminal hid his true nature and deceived wise men—who, like angels, cannot penetrate hypocrisy. In Austen's work the ordeal is twofold. It is not Wickham who singlehandedly misleads Elizabeth Bennet in *Pride and Prejudice*. It is Elizabeth's declaration about Darcy, "I think him very disagreeable" (p. 77), that prompts Wickham to fill in a dark picture of that hero. So also in *Emma*, Frank Churchill does not dupe Miss Woodhouse into supposing he loves her. Emma imposes on his character the assumption that flatters herself. Willoughby, in *Sense and Sensibility*, and Henry Crawford, in *Mansfield Park*, both cheat themselves, expecting to receive casual amusement from girls who end by winning their hearts, and whose loss punishes them for their depravity.

When the villains get their way, the implications remain similar. Most of the victims, in Austen's novels, are not simply ruined by malefactors. They contribute to their own delinquency. The villain (Willoughby, Crawford, Elliot) serves their corrupted impulses.[2]

Not only is the inwardness of Austen's stories the source of their fascination; it also determines her narrative technique. By making the obstacles internal rather than external, Austen drove her genius to invent ways of disclosing them, because an ignorant character could hardly reveal what he did not know. Among

2. Cf. *Sense and Sensibility*, p. 322; *Mansfield Park*, p. 468; and *Persuasion*, p. 250. Edward Ferrars, in *Sense and Sensibility*, and Georgiana Darcy, in *Pride and Prejudice*, are genuine victims of seducers.

such devices the simplest is indeed explicit statement; and Austen often tells us outright what is happening in the heart or brain of her creatures.

Elizabeth Bennet's mother, says her maker, "was a woman of mean understanding, little information, and uncertain temper" (p. 5). The reader understands at once why Mrs. Bennet has not kept her husband's affection. Of Mrs. Norris in *Mansfield Park*, Austen writes that "her love of money was equal to her love of directing" (p. 8); and the alternation of bossiness with avarice explains much of Mrs. Norris's evildoing. In *Persuasion*, Austen blurts out the truth about Sir Walter Elliot: "Vanity was the beginning and the end of Sir Walter Elliot's character; vanity of person and of situation" (p. 4). It becomes obvious why the unprepossessing Mrs. Clay could hope to snare him with flattery.

When these judgments emanate from the author, they are invariably to be trusted; and the character's behavior never fails to exemplify them. When they derive from a speaker in the novel, we must scrutinize them skeptically. In *Mansfield Park*, Edmund Bertram's praise of Mary Crawford tells us more about him than about her; and in *Persuasion*, Lady Russell's encomium of Mr. Elliot (pp. 146–47) is a sly comment on her distrust of Wentworth.

Contrary to the assumptions of many critics, the flat, explicit remark in no way restrains Austen from dramatic illustration of the character through dialogue, gesture, and of course conduct. In scene after scene she quietly implies the judgment she has openly delivered; or else she illustrates it first and then points her meaning, as with John Thorpe in *Northanger Abbey*—who boasts, exaggerates, and contradicts himself until Catherine Morland cannot tell what to make of him; whereupon Austen audibly declares that Miss Morland "had not been brought up to understand the propensities of a rattle, nor to know to how many idle assertions and impudent falsehoods the excess of vanity will lead" (p. 65). Even more blunt is an assertion (in *Persuasion*) about Elizabeth Elliot: at Bath, after talking to Wentworth, Anne Elliot feels blissful. Her snobbish sister is also blissful, on account of Lady Dalrymple's company. Austen comments, "[It] would be an insult to the nature of Anne's felicity, to draw any comparison between it and her sister's; the origin of one all selfish vanity, of the other all generous attachment" (p. 185).

But a reader must guard himself against inferring too much from an appearance of explicitness. The novelist often tests our powers of discrimination by letting a highly sympathetic character deliver a wrong judgment or a false interpretation of motives. She likes to catch her hero or heroine in a blunder. Consequently, the best people can mislead us. When Elinor Dashwood, in *Sense and Sensibility*, looks at a plait of hair in Edward Ferrars's ring, Austen reports, "That the hair was her own, she instantaneously felt . . . satisfied" (p. 98); and few readers fail to accept her opinion at this point. But Edward's embarrassment warns us to be doubtful; and we discover finally that Elinor was wrong (p. 365). Emma Woodhouse, of course, is so often mistaken that we learn to distrust her. But even the judicious Anne Elliot, in *Persuasion*, goes astray in dealing with her cousin Mr. Elliot. Not only does she grossly overvalue him; she also feels confident that he is pursuing her sister. Actually, however, when Elliot is not trying to detach Sir Walter from Mrs. Clay, he is on the trail of Anne herself.

On the other hand, the fact that Austen has labeled a character stupid does not imply that she repudiates all his opinions, any more than she backs all those of the person whom she invites us to admire (especially when the topic relates to the motions of the heart). Austen will ridicule the triteness of a remark without objecting to its substance, or she will expose the insincerity of a speaker while agreeing with his statement.

When Mrs. Bennet objects to Darcy's criticism of a country neighborhood as socially confining, she says that London has "no great advantage over the country . . . except the shops and public places" (*Pride and Prejudice*, p. 43). A British scholar assumes that Austen cannot agree with the silly woman;[3] but we

3. Frank Bradbrook, *Jane Austen and Her Predecessors* (Cambridge, England: Cambridge University Press, 1966), p. 41.

have no reason to think so. We only know the sentiment is threadbare and the speaker is fatuous. In the same novel, when the self-important Mr. Collins says he regards the office of a clergyman as "equal in point of dignity with the highest rank in the kingdom" (p. 97), Austen asks us to smile at a lack of originality, not an error. Or to take a subtler example, when Mr. Collins states that he considers music "as a very innocent diversion, and perfectly compatible with the profession of a clergyman" (p. 101), his words are evidently a parody of William Gilpin's preface to *Observations on Cumberland and Westmoreland*.[4] But this does not imply that Austen disagreed with Gilpin's views on landscape, for we know she adopted them—even as she also delighted in music.

So the explicitness of the novelist is sometimes only apparent, and at other times is a game played with an audience. By sounding blunt and outspoken in many of her judgments, Austen entices unwary readers into assuming that she is essentially straightforward. She benumbs our critical faculties and screens from observation the kind of legerdemain that she practices with the relations between Emma Woodhouse and Frank Churchill. Who among us is so acute as to notice when the author merely withholds her opinion of a character from us? Who is so acute as to infer that in such cases she is letting us mislead ourselves?

But it remains true that when Austen does plainly set forth her judgment, it is—as I have said—quite reliable. We must appreciate the conciseness of emphasis in these giveaways (which a playwright can rarely afford).[5] But emphasis never calls our keenest imagination into play. Neither would it prevent the novelist from letting us know the political opinions of Mr. Bennet, the religious doctrines of Mrs. Norris, or the sexual habits of Sir Walter Elliot.

There are of course less direct means of bringing out the

4. Ibid., p. 57.
5. A playwright can distinguish his own voice from that of his characters only by undramatic or improbable devices: a prologue, a narrator, a chorus, a conventionally trustworthy soliloquy.

hidden processes and motives in a novel. Perhaps the simplest is to let one person tattle on another. Thus in *Sense and Sensibility*, Colonel Brandon informs the heroine, Elinor Dashwood, of the vicious nature of Willoughby, who has abused her sister (pp. 209–10); and in *Persuasion*, the invalid Mrs. Smith tells the heroine about the misdeeds of her suitor and cousin Mr. Elliot (pp. 199–211). This is how the reader learns why in fact Willoughby lost Marianne, and why Mr. Elliot lost his cousin Anne: namely, the men's debauched impulses got in the way of their enlightened judgment.

Such detailed revelations, in dialogue or by letter, have an old-fashioned atmosphere, like the interpolated tales of Fielding's novels, or the éclaircissement of *The Vicar of Wakefield*. They seem out of keeping with the probabilities of the rest of the story. Besides, not only would they fail to inhibit the discussion of politics, religion, or sexual passion; they would facilitate it. Precisely through such old-fashioned autobiographical tales, in *Sense and Sensibility*, *Pride and Prejudice*, and *Persuasion*, Austen takes us into the ugly concreteness of lust and greed.

A quieter but far busier route for the release of latent purposes is through the novelist's favorite device, narrative contrast. Like many storytellers and playwrights, Austen conceives her plots in terms of moral parallels and antitheses hierarchically arranged, with the main patterns shadowed by subordinate designs. But hers are subtle and evocative to a degree seldom reached by other writers. In *Pride and Prejudice* we start with Darcy's pride balanced against Elizabeth Bennet's prejudice. This contrast is set off by the easy harmony of Jane Bennet and Charles Bingley on the one side, and the bleak mésalliance of plain Charlotte Lucas and the obsequious Mr. Collins on the other; and around these figures move such epiphenomena as the opposition of Elizabeth's health and candor to Anne de Burgh's sickliness and Caroline Bingley's malice. By pairing characters and actions, Austen endlessly brings out virtues, faults, and motives that would otherwise lie hidden. Thus Mr. Bennet's intelligence is parallel to that of Mr. Gardiner, his brother-in-law, but his irresponsibility is exposed by the latter's active wisdom.

Though Austen's predominant method is contrast, that method receives peculiar complications. For instance, the contrast is often incomplete and waits to be filled out by the reader. In *Emma*, Frank Churchill is secretive while Mr. Knightley is open; Churchill is impulsive while Knightley is deliberate. These differences are clear. But the reader must surmise for himself that since Knightley feels deeply attracted by the spirit of Emma, Churchill must be deeply attracted by the physical beauty of Jane Fairfax. Sure enough, when Churchill tells Emma of his love for Jane, he dwells upon her appearance:

> Did you ever see such a skin?—such smoothness! such delicacy! —and yet without being actually fair.—One cannot call her fair. It is a most uncommon complexion, with her dark eyelashes and hair—a most distinguishing complexion!—So peculiarly the lady in it.—Just enough colour for beauty.   (p. 478)

So also in *Mansfield Park* Austen sets off Edmund Bertram against Henry Crawford. Edmund inclines to be blunt (pp. 50, 94); Crawford is witty and gallant. Edmund is deeply rooted; Crawford dislikes being confined to one place and one set of friends (p. 41). It is left to the reader to infer that if Edmund is a constant wooer, with eyes only for the lady he loves, Crawford will be distractable and relax his attention when Fanny is absent. Yet that is what happens. For all his vows of fidelity, Crawford cannot resist the challenge of Maria's ambivalence when he meets her after her marriage; and so he runs away with Mrs. Rushworth and loses Miss Price.

Not only are Austen's contrasts systematically incomplete. They are also moral. In *Pride and Prejudice*, Darcy and Bingley are not opposed to one another as fat and thin or dark and fair but as reserved and sociable, deliberate and impulsive. In Austen's system of implicit contrasts, if Bingley is open and active in his attentions to Jane Bennet, we may assume that Darcy will be cautious in advancing toward her sister's heart.

Thanks to the use of moral contrast, Austen can infuse

subtle implications into devices that do not essentially involve them. For example, in her narrative tradition, speeches and gestures are normally completed. If they are broken off, the storyteller implies that a strong emotion is the cause, and the emotion as such is in general obvious. In the *Aeneid* when Neptune is angry with the winds for causing a storm he has not asked for, he breaks off a sentence starting *Quos ego*—and the listener knows he is angry (*Aeneid* I, 135).

Austen always implies hidden motives with moral overtones when she interrupts an action. In *Emma*, when Jane Fairfax refuses to continue a game of anagrams, Austen implies not only that she is embarrassed but that Frank Churchill has been indelicate and shown himself unworthy of her (pp. 347–49). Our inference depends of course on the steady contrast drawn between his assurance and her refinement. A more subtle and economical example is Eleanor Tilney's interruption of herself in *Northanger Abbey*. At the end of a friendly conversation Catherine Morland asks her whether she will be at the ball the next day. "Perhaps we—yes, I think we certainly shall," says Miss Tilney (p. 73). The reader should understand that she has just recognized Catherine's fondness for her brother, and that she wisely wishes to encourage it. The reason for her feeling is that both girls are simple, truthful, and modest, a congruity that sets them off against Isabella Thorpe.

How far Austen could carry such didactic art, we may judge from the elaborate episode, in *Emma*, of Knightley's almost kissing the heroine's hand.[6] He takes her hand, presses it, and is certainly on the point of carrying it to his lips when he suddenly lets go (pp. 385–86). The reason, we may infer, is that he feels he has no right to seem so affectionate because Emma is (he mistakenly believes) attached to Frank Churchill. Again, we can make the judgment—and admire his delicacy—because of a contrast regularly drawn between Knightley and Churchill.

Yet the most striking and pervasive feature of Austen's contrasts is that they are metonymic. When a person is connected

6. Austen adapted the episode from a similar one in Burney's *Camilla*. See Bradbrook, pp. 100–102.

with a visible element, that element takes on the character of the person. For example, in *Pride and Prejudice*, when Jane Bennet and Charles Bingley exchange views on card games, they find they both like vingt-un better than the game of commerce (p. 23). Now it happens that in commerce the players barter for cards, while in vingt-un they keep their own. Jane and Bingley are people whose attachment is deep and enduring; their dislike of barter reflects the trait. In *Northanger Abbey*, the flirtatious Isabella plays commerce while acting a faithless part (pp. 89–90). In *Mansfield Park*, Mary Crawford's zest for the game of speculation—in which the players buy trumps from one another—discloses her rash, ambitious nature. "No cold prudence for me," she says (p. 243).

It is easy to fit landed property into the scheme of implicit and metonymic contrasts. Bingley lives in a rented house, even as he shows his agreeable manners in public places. Darcy clings to his ancestral estate and is most himself at home. Lady Catherine de Burgh has the marks of a careful guardian of her estate; but they reveal her egoism just as General Tilney's pride in his good taste (*Northanger Abbey*, pp. 162, 165–66, 175) betokens not moral integrity but a confusion of aesthetic with spiritual values. Contrary to the views of several critics, Austen does not make manners, taste, or good stewardship, in themselves, a sure sign of virtue.

We observe a similar use of physical attributes. When Darcy must talk about Elizabeth Bennet's outward appearance, he dwells on her eyes, which are of course the windows of the soul; for her spirit is what charms him. But in *Emma*, as we have heard, Frank Churchill spends his raptures on Jane Fairfax's complexion, the most superficial and mutable aspect of her body.

There was nothing unconscious about Austen's handling of this theme, as one may learn from its elaboration in *Mansfield Park*. Here, Edmund Bertram relays to Fanny Price his father's praise of her; and it is instructive that Sir Thomas should have drawn Edmund's attention to the girl's appearance, while Edmund himself sees her "beauty of mind" (pp. 197–98). Surfaces mean too much to Sir Thomas, and this failing is what lets him connive at his daughter's monstrous marriage to Rushworth. When the corrupt Henry Crawford talks to his sister about Fanny, he takes the same line, and praises her for being "absolutely pretty" (pp. 229–30). The implications of such judgments become explicit when Fanny receives a letter from Mary Crawford about Edmund Bertram. Mary tells how her friends in London have praised Edmund's "gentleman-like appearance," and dwells on one lady's declaration that she knows "but three men in town who have so good a person, height, and air." Fanny immediately condemns Mary as a "woman who could speak of him, and speak only of his appearance!—What an unworthy attachment!" (pp. 417–18).

It becomes a sign of Austen's genius that almost any article associated with an individual may work as a surrogate for that person. One of the most delicate and beautiful examples is the scene following Darcy's first proposal in *Pride and Prejudice*. Elizabeth receives a letter that dissolves her false impressions of him. She reconsiders her own character and that of the abominable Wickham. In a sentence that may or may not represent a thrust of irony on the novelist's part, Elizabeth decides that her error was due to vanity:

> Had I been in love, I could not have been more wretchedly blind. But vanity, not love, has been my folly. (p. 208)

Are we to invert this apparent self-discovery and think that Elizabeth had been unconsciously in love with Darcy when he proposed, and that the humiliating terms of the proposal transformed latent affection into conscious anger? Going over the letter in her mind, Elizabeth concludes that essential justice lay on Darcy's side. When she returns to the vicarage, she learns that both Darcy and his cousin Colonel Fitzwilliam had called while she was out. Fitzwilliam's manners had charmed her, but now, Austen says,

> Elizabeth could but just *affect* concern in missing him; she really rejoiced at it. Colonel Fitzwilliam was no longer an object. She could think only of her letter. (p. 209)

That is to say, she could think only of Darcy, with whom at this point she is certainly in love.

Now it would be hard indeed to import politics or religion into the scheme of metonymic contrast. Those occupations presuppose organized sects and parties external to the individual and his morality. They rest on strong polarities that cut across private good and evil. Historically, sects or parties must claim moral superiority; and they must be pitted against one another as such. One could not possibly bring them into the subtle symmetries of Austen's design without swamping it.

So also the novelist does not dwell on aspects of life concerning which the moral judgment must be self-evident: naked avarice or gluttony, violent anger, open atheism. These are too easy to identify and too easy to blame. Her method of metonymic contrast would be pointless with them.

When Austen uses this method of contrast diachronically, or over a period of time, it produces those reversals of expectation and insight that make a staple of comic plots: in *Pride and Prejudice*, Mrs. Bennet's judging Darcy as worthless just before she learns that Elizabeth will marry him, and as faultless just afterwards (pp. 374, 378); in *Emma*, Knightley's change of heart toward Churchill when he discovers that Emma does not love the man (p. 483).

Austen refines this ancient device in two ways. In her fictions, it rises from self-knowledge; and it also takes on moral implications, at least for the main characters. In *Pride and Prejudice* an example is the difference between the shameless Wickham's cardparty conversation about Darcy when he first meets Elizabeth (pp. 77–84) and their tête-à-tête on the same subject after Wickham has married the runaway Lydia (pp. 327–29). The young husband staggers the reader by showing the same engaging manners and self-possession in the drastically altered circumstances; only Elizabeth has changed; and in this case, a persistence implies moral corruption, whereas change implies wisdom. The device becomes explicit in *Mansfield Park*, when Henry Crawford returns to the Bertrams' after Maria's marriage and speaks (the author says) as if he had "no embarrassing remembrance" to affect his spirits (p. 224).

Sometimes the diachronic contrasts are enriched by a scenic parallelism. The same arrangements reappear with different evocations. When Mr. Collins proposes marriage to Elizabeth Bennet in the breakfast parlor of her father's house (27 November; pp. 104–9), he dwells on her disadvantages but assumes that she will accept him; and the effect is comic. At the same time, he foreshadows the posture of Mr. Darcy several months later (9 April; pp. 189–93), when that great gentleman proposes marriage to Elizabeth in Mr. Collins's own house and also dwells on her disadvantages but assumes that she will accept him; only the effect is then high drama with deep moral implications.

So when Lady Catherine tells Elizabeth that Darcy must not marry her (3 October; pp. 353–58), the two women are walking in a grove at Longbourne; and this had been exactly the position of Elizabeth with her ladyship's nephew, in the grove at Rosings six months earlier (p. 195), when he gave her a letter detailing the same objections—only in the earlier episode the near-elopement of Darcy's sister came under discussion, and in the later episode the actual elopement of Elizabeth's sister.

To represent her minor figures, Austen tends to employ not metonymy but synecdoche, or the substitution of a part for the whole. One aspect of the character does duty for the entire person. Mrs. Bennet incarnates a passion for marrying off her daughters, even as Mrs. Allen in *Northanger Abbey* is reduced to an obsession with clothes. This reductive method of characterization may sound like the tradition of the comedy of humors but is closer to Pope's theory of a ruling passion. The effect is not flat or stereotype because the element is conceived as governing other motives and not replacing them. Mrs. Bennet's favorite child, for example, is Lydia, who subordinates all decent occupations to the pursuit of males. Her least favorite is Elizabeth, who refuses two proposals of marriage. Lady Catherine, in *Pride and Prejudice*, does little but order other people about. In conversation she alternates questions with commands. But such a reduction does not prevent her from showing ample hospitality to her parson's guests, the reason being that she may thereby have a more numerous body of submissive companions. Although the scenes that follow come close to burlesque, they also illustrate genuine principles of psychology. So also it is no accident that the prudent Charlotte Lucas, daughter of a man consumed by social ambition, should find a husband who cringes before a title of honor.

Sir Walter Scott makes a vivid contrast to Austen in his methods, because his plots depend on violent, external action; his stories are shaped by political principle and religious doctrine; and his contrasts are metaphoric or symbolic. Even a performance of music or a choice of reading must, with Scott's technique, be subordinated to historical issues. In *Waverley*, when Flora MacIvor sings, the novelist arranges the occasion to illustrate the tradition of Scottish Jacobite patriotism both in landscape and in language (chapter 22). Flora herself becomes almost an abstraction. By a ruthless metaphoric symbolism, she can appear only as the spirit of an ideology.

Austen avoids metaphor or symbolism in her art. In Scott's *Waverley* when the hero dresses himself in the tartan, he takes on its associations; it does not reflect his; for Scott uses the tartan as a metaphor for Jacobitism. But in Austen's stories, a thing, a gesture, an occupation seldom has moral significance or general meaning apart from the individual to whom it belongs. Austen can transform all the circumstances of common life into implicit moral comment: space, time, landscape, architecture, furniture. What she will not do is to attribute independent symbolic meaning to those circumstances. Darcy's attention to books indicates the depth of his moral and intellectual culture. Wentworth's indifference to books, in *Persuasion*, makes a contrast to the reading habits of his shallow friend Benwick, who replaces true feeling with literary sentiment. Games, books, articles of clothing, are in themselves neither good nor bad for Austen; they stand for no general principle until connected with a particular character. When Mary Bennet or Anne Elliot plays the piano, the performance takes on the color of her nature. With Mary

impatience with her humble friend is perhaps the underside of her patience with Mr. Woodhouse.

Austen's reliance on moral metonymy and synecdoche in a scheme of ironic parallels and contrasts will account for another difference between her own narrative style and that of Scott. This is their use of concrete particularity in description. By "concrete particularity," I mean the representation of persons, objects, etc., through sensuous details so peculiar to them that the reader feels he could identify the unique specimen in experience, if only by two or three distinctive marks. (I do not mean the use of generic epithets or the listing of items or the reporting of impressions provoked by the subject.)

Contrary to the assumption of many critics of the novel, such descriptions are rare in great novels of the period 1720–1820, though common in the works of Scott, Mrs. Gaskell, and George Eliot. Where they may seem to exist in proto-novels like *Pilgrim's Progress* or *Gulliver's Travels*, inspection will show that the details are symbolic, or that they allude to historical subjects outside the fiction itself. It will also be found that concrete particularity (as in the novels of Smollett and Edgeworth) usually finds its application proper to low subjects, to comic butts and satirical targets, to themes of humorous fantasy, but not to elevated, dignified, sympathetic subjects. I suppose this literary instinct begins with the natural tendency to avert one's eyes from an object of respect or awe, and that dignity often collapses under a close scrutiny of its sensuous aspects.

In this matter the difference between Austen and Scott is enormous. He delights in external action, representing the physical features of his characters, their clothes, houses, and the landscapes around them, in vivid detail. She weakens these effects. Out of scores of possible examples, I may instance the arrival of Fanny Price at her father's house in Portsmouth (*Mansfield Park*, pp. 376–82) and Frank Osbaldistone's arrival at his uncle's seat in Northumberland (*Rob Roy*, chapters 5–6). Austen focuses her account on Fanny's emotions, responses, disappointments, as she discovers the confusion, noise, and crowding of her family's circumstances—above all, the thoughtless indifference to herself. The novelist supplies only the faintest hints of the appearance of things, just enough to lead one into Fanny's impressions. Scott has the same kind of family to deal with: large, vulgar, noisy, self-absorbed, and hopelessly confused. Since the story is told in the first person, it would be easy for him to render the external by the internal, as Austen does. But he uses Frank's feelings as a pretext for describing (splendidly, of course) the landscape, the building, the furniture, the features of many people, and their clothing. I think his description of Rashleigh alone gives us a greater number of concrete details than Austen provides for all the characters of *Mansfield Park* together.

Yet while Austen directs her whole system of contrasts toward elucidating the moral substance of her principal figures, it is remarkable how vague Scott can be about his protagonists. The moral character of Waverley, Staunton (in *The Heart of Midlothian*), or Latimer (in *Redgauntlet*) is either evasive or unfixed. Although Henry Morton's moderation embodies the essential doctrine of *Old Mortality*, it looks very much like fence-sitting; and near the end, when the extremists on either side of him destroy themselves, Morton himself almost dissolves into an emblem of an abstraction. Perhaps it could hardly be otherwise if Scott wished to leave us with a deep impression of Morton as a bridge between the old world and the new.

Austen, of course, rarely alludes to the appearance of her characters in concrete detail. The very act of focused representation seems to have meaning for her. Either the person singled out is blameworthy, or the one producing the description is misbehaving. Austen quickly sketches Henry Tilney in *Northanger Abbey*: about twenty-five, rather tall, nearly handsome, with a pleasant face and an intelligent eye (p. 25). Most of these features are not distinguishing marks but impressions of the personality upon an observer. However, Isabella Thorpe, who is shallow and preoccupied with complexions, extracts more concrete detail (still not Flaubertian) from Catherine: "brown skin, with dark eyes, and rather dark hair" (p. 42). Her concern with such data—and especially with complexions—

puzzles Catherine and exposes Isabella. In *Pride and Prejudice* the only minute account we hear of Elizabeth Bennet emanates from the malicious Caroline Bingley in an attempt to weaken Darcy's growing attachment to her (pp. 270–71). In *Emma*, it is the jealous heroine who provides a list of the features of Jane Fairfax—partly because Emma dislikes her and partly because her appearance is what attracts Frank Churchill (pp. 166–67, 478–79).

Austen's refusal to stare at her creatures also reflects a general disposition to avoid details that cannot involve moral choice, such as the color of one's hair. In *Sense and Sensibility*, Elinor tries to see the color of the hair set in Edward Ferrars's ring, because it might be her own; yet Austen keeps from telling us what the color is, or indeed the actual color of Elinor's hair! (pp. 98–99). Nevertheless, in the same novel Austen does describe the selfish, arrogant Mrs. Ferrars with surprising particularity:

> a little, thin woman, upright, even to formality, in her figure, and serious, even to sourness, in her aspect. Her complexion was sallow; and her features small, without beauty, and naturally without expression; but a lucky contraction of the brow had rescued her countenance from the disgrace of insipidity, by giving it the strong characters of pride and ill nature. She was not a woman of many words: for, unlike people in general, she proportioned them to the number of her ideas. . . . (p. 232)

But Mrs. Ferrars's arrogance is one of the two great obstacles to the marriage of Austen's heroine. Her ill nature gives Austen grounds for satiric particularity.

Persuasion offers one an opportunity to compare a sympathetic character with an evildoer as subjects for description. Here Austen introduces her protagonist as follows:

> A few years before, Anne Elliot had been a very pretty girl, but her bloom had vanished early; and as even in its height, her father had found little to admire in her, (so totally different were her delicate features and mild dark eyes from his own); there could be nothing in them now that she was faded and thin, to excite his esteem. (p. 6)

The author uses a few vague references to physical features as a device for setting the daughter's moral nature against the father's. She gives us the general impression that Anne would make on a kind observer but also sees her through the father's unkind vision. The young woman had delicate features, dark eyes, and a thin body. Was the nose turned up? the hair brown? the eyes black? Of concrete particulars we learn little, certainly not enough to recognize the person.

One of the scoundrels in *Persuasion* receives a different sort of representation. I quote:

> Mrs. Clay had freckles, and a projecting tooth, and a clumsy wrist, which [Sir Walter Elliot] was continually making severe remarks upon, in her absence; but she was young, and certainly altogether well-looking, and possessed, in an acute mind and assiduous pleasing manners, infinitely more dangerous attractions than any merely personal might have been.[10]   (p. 24)

Along with the impression that Mrs. Clay makes on Anne's father, along with a general indication of her appearance, Austen gives us surprisingly sharp details: freckles, a projecting tooth, and a clumsy wrist. Whoever studies Austen with attention will learn that not only in *Persuasion* but generally, the novelist suppresses concrete detail in descriptions of her sympathetic characters but may supply it for persons of ambiguous morality. In this way she transforms an elementary technical demand of prose narrative into an implication of moral judgment.

By invoking her large patterns of metonymic and ironic contrast, Austen can exert pressure not only on incomplete speeches or gestures but on a single word—or the absence of a word. Thus in *Pride and Prejudice* during one of the conversations at Hunsdon which lead up to his proposal of marriage, Darcy disagrees with Elizabeth about the distance of this village from Longbourn, which she considers great. "Any thing beyond the very neighbourhood of Longbourn, I suppose, would appear far," says Darcy (p. 179). He shows a faint smile which, Austen

---

10. It is of course ironical that Sir Walter, obsessed with superficial beauty, might be attracted to a woman with faulty features; and this irony is a cause of Austen's particularity.

tells us, "Elizabeth fancied she understood; he must be supposing her to be thinking of Jane and Netherfield." Of course, Darcy's slight gesture tells us that he must be thinking of Elizabeth and his own estate at Pemberley, which is remote indeed from Longbourn.

We can infer so much because by this point the scheme of polarities between Elizabeth's modesty and Darcy's assurance is well established, and because Austen has indicated that in the region of Wickham, Darcy, and herself, Elizabeth does not know anyone's heart, least of all her own. With the unreliability of the heroine established, the author's word "fancied" gains its weight. It separates the novelist from her creature, and we have therefore to doubt that Elizabeth is right in her inference. If, however, Jane is not in Darcy's mind, Elizabeth should be.

It is through such indirection that we may establish a bridge between the art of the novelist and the social order in which her genius flourished. Sex, religion, and politics do color Austen's themes after all, though in a very different manner from Scott's use of them. To start, one may fairly tease an attitude toward government out of the novels. For instance, it is true that Austen conspicuously avoids political controversy. In *Northanger Abbey* critics have observed how Tilney, who delights in conversation, stops talking when his lecture on landscape carries him into a digression on the British constitution:

> . . . by an easy transition from a piece of rocky fragment and the withered oak which he had placed near its summit, to oaks in general, for forests, the inclosure of them, waste lands, crown lands and government, he shortly found himself arrived at politics; and from politics, it was an easy step to silence. (p. 111)

Again in *Sense and Sensibility* we detect something like a sneer when Austen alludes to the ambition of the hero's mother and sister:

> They wanted him to make a fine figure in the world in some manner or other. His mother wished to interest him in political concerns, to get him into parliament, or to see him connected with some of the great men of the day. Mrs. John Dashwood wished it likewise; but in the mean while, till one of those

superior blessings could be attained, it would have quieted her
ambition to see him driving a barouche.   (pp. 15–16)

The interchangeability of a barouche and a political career is
no slip of the pen; and Austen's irony suggests the traditional
attitude of the gentry, always suspicious of men at the center
of government. In the same novel it is the affected Mr. Palmer
who busies himself standing for Parliament (p. 113); and his
fatuous wife suggests that he could not visit Willoughby because the latter was, as she says, "in the opposition" (p. 114).
It is obvious what Austen thinks of people who arrange their
friendships according to their politics.

In *Mansfield Park*, Sir Thomas Bertram is in Parliament;
but Austen mentions the fact only in the most casual way and
as a burden rather than a distinction (p. 20). In this novel it is
certainly a mark against Mary Crawford that she should imag-
ine Edmund might rise to distinction by going into Parliament
(p. 214).

Beyond this point, however, the novelist had no means of
drawing political philosophy into her grand scheme unless she
set moral labels on political sides. And yet one may smell a quasi-
political implication in her social doctrine. Austen, like all
important novelists from 1720 to 1820, showed little interest in
the urban middle class as an ideal social type. Even Defoe assumed that a sane bourgeois naturally aspired to the condition
of a landed country gentleman.

For Austen, the social class that mattered was indeed the
gentry, rising no higher than baronets. It is notable that peers
never have a role in her work, except for the dowager Viscountess Dalrymple in *Persuasion*.[11] Although clergymen
abound in the novels, bishops do not exist. Presentations to Aus-

11. In *Northanger Abbey*, Miss Tilney marries a young man who
unexpectedly comes into a peerage; but he was not raised as a lord (p.
251). In *Sense and Sensibility* the arrogant Mrs. Ferrars wishes her son
Edward to marry the daughter of a lord (p. 224). In *Pride and Prejudice*,
Colonel Fitzwilliam is the younger son of a peer and indicates that he
must marry for money (pp. 183–84). In *Mansfield Park* the contemptible
Mr. Yates is the younger son of a lord (p. 121).

ten's livings are made by lay patrons. So also, while we meet lawyers, we meet no titled judges.

Austen, in fact, accepts a social ideology that goes back to the seventeenth century, one which cuts across divisions based on the means of economic production or the source of one's income. In this ideology the church is not united against any other category of economic, political or social types; neither are the landed classes or the bourgeoisie. On the contrary, all these strata bifurcate at the same point: the gentry against the peerage, the lower clergy against the bishops, the tradesmen of the provincial towns against the great merchants and bankers in London.

At the same time, such categories are connected across economic lines. The gentry supply the members of the beneficed clergy from their own families and present them to the family livings. Younger sons who do not enter the church may have commissions bought for them in the army or navy, unless they choose to follow the law or to find a post in the East India Company. The provincial tradesmen depend on and are aligned with the squires.

From the era of Dryden's poem on "John Driden" (his namesake cousin) to that of Austen's *Persuasion*, the gentry's independence of the court served as a moral principle. It is no accident that in *Northanger Abbey* the reprehensible General Tilney should have an old friend who happens to be a marquis (pp. 139, 224), or that in *Persuasion* the frivolous Sir Walter Elliot should fawn upon a viscountess (pp. 148–50, 184–85). Coming away from *Pride and Prejudice*, some readers commit the mistake of placing Lady Catherine in the peerage. She is of course an earl's daughter, but only a knight's widow. When her ladyship's sister's son—Darcy—tells Elizabeth Bennet about his childhood, he gives no praise to his maternal line. On the contrary, it is explicitly his father that Darcy describes as "all that was benevolent and amiable" (p. 369).

So also when Austen satirizes Sir William Lucas, a prosperous tradesman who received a knighthood while serving as lord mayor (*Pride and Prejudice*, p. 18), she describes him in a pun as having grown "courteous"; and by a kind of synecdoche she reduces his inoffensive character to the itch of seeming at ease in the royal court (p. 160). We last hear Sir William attributing to Darcy, who is happiest in rural Derbyshire, his own desire to meet frequently at St. James's (p. 384).

If we retreat from literature to biography, we may be sure that Austen had personal experience of noble lords. It is possible however that life imitated art; for when she described the "very pleasing" manners of Lord Craven, she said, "The little flaw of having a mistress now living with him at Ashdown Park, seems to be the only unpleasing circumstance about him."[12] The sarcasm hints that Austen had a deeper awareness of sexual appetite than is explicit in her novels. In fact, just as she seems after all to suggest certain political and social doctrines, so also she reveals views on passion and courtship which her novels may be said to inculcate (by implication only) as doctrines. This will be manifest if we compare her novels with those of Scott.

In *Waverley* (published the same year as *Mansfield Park*), when the hero finds himself passing many hours with the beautiful Rose Bradwardine, Scott assures us that Waverley is not falling in love with the girl. Familiarity obstructs romantic passion, says Scott: "the very intimacy of their intercourse prevented his feeling for her other sentiments than those of a brother for an amiable and accomplished sister" (chapter 14). Again in *Redgauntlet* (published ten years later), when Darsie Latimer discovers that the girl in the green mantle, who had occupied his reveries since they first met, shows no objection to kissing him on command, he is disgusted: "It was in vain," says Scott, "that . . . he endeavoured to coax back, if I may so express myself, that delightful dream of ardent and tender passion" (chapter 18 of part 2).[13]

---

12. *Letters*, p. 106.

13. *Redgauntlet* (London: J. M. Dent, Everyman's Library, 1908), p. 349; cf. p. 345. Of course, Scott recognized the validity of Austen's position (cf. discussion below, and *Redgauntlet*, p. 350); but he did not choose to dramatize it.

In Austen's mature novels nothing conduces more to love than neighborhood and close acquaintance. In *Sense and Sensibility*, Marianne is brought to love and marry Colonel Brandon through his proximity and through a conspiracy of her family to bring the two together. Then his own goodness and his deep attachment to her do their work (p. 378). In *Pride and Prejudice* the unfolding of Bingley's love for Jane Bennet is interrupted simply by his being removed from her region. In *Persuasion*, Benwick and Louisa Musgrove fall in love by living in the same house while she recuperates from her fall. In *Mansfield Park*, Edmund and Fanny build their engagement on just that "warm and sisterly regard" (p. 470) which Scott eliminates as a source of romantic love. Indeed, to sum up Austen's doctrine, one need only reverse Scott's analysis of the relation between Rose Bradwardine and Edward Waverley:

> [She] had not precisely the sort of beauty or merit, which captivates a romantic imagination in early youth. She was too frank, too confiding, too kind; amiable qualities, undoubtedly, but destructive of the marvellous, with which a youth of imagination delights to dress the empress of his affections.
>
> (*Waverley*, chapter 14)

In *Northanger Abbey*, if anything attracts Henry Tilney to Catherine Morland, it is her frankness, confidence, and kindness (p. 243).

So I am not persuaded by those critics who judge the endings of *Northanger Abbey* and *Mansfield Park* to be mere games with convention, or deliberately playful windings-up of essentially comic plots. They are those things, of course. But they are also hints of Austen's earthy view of passion and courtship. Given proximity, familiarity, and persistence, a set of good qualities on one side will respond to a set of good qualities on the other, so long as an impulse begins somewhere. This is why cunning hypocrisy is so dangerous. When a man who appears to be an eligible partner plays up to the expectations of an unworldly young lady, he is likely to succeed, as Willoughby succeeds with Marianne in *Sense and Sensibility*. The best shield against such an intrigue is a previous commitment to a better man. R. W. Chapman pointed out places in *Emma* in which Austen hints that the heroine is thinking of Mr. Knightley without our being told so explicitly.[14] In all these, Frank Churchill is either near her or in her thoughts. We may infer, from Austen's system of contrasts, that he is not simply opposed to Knightley but that Emma is protected from Churchill's deliberate campaign by her unconscious love for Knightley.

A subtler example occurs in *Persuasion*. Anne Elliot reflects on her feelings toward Mr. Elliot, who seems a thoroughly appropriate suitor; and she decides that his great fault is not being "open." Austen says, "She prized the frank, the openhearted, the eager character beyond all others" (p. 161). We may infer that Wentworth is at the edge of her mind. But we may also infer that it was the attachment to him which saved her from Elliot; for later Anne admits to herself that she might just possibly have been induced to marry her cousin (p. 211).

Austen puts it all explicitly in *Mansfield Park*, when she explains where Fanny found the strength to resist Henry Crawford:

> [Although] there doubtless are such unconquerable young ladies of eighteen (or one should not read about them) as are never to be persuaded into love against their judgment by all that talent, manner, attention and flattery can do, I have no inclination to believe Fanny one of them, or to think that with so much tenderness of disposition, and so much taste as belonged to her, she could have escaped heart-whole from the courtship [of a man like Crawford] had not her affection been engaged elsewhere. (p. 231)

Outside courtship, the same circumstances operate. An unprincipled man who finds himself near an interested woman will (Austen implies) deliver himself to her. In *Pride and Prejudice*, Lydia lays no snare to seduce Wickham, and he does not pine for her as an object of irresistible passion. He was in the habit; she was convenient and interested; off they ran. In *Persuasion*, Mrs. Clay exhibits her availability to Mr. Elliot by sending him on an errand when she cannot arrange for him to accompany

14. *Emma*, pp. 491–92.

her in the rain (pp. 174–75). She meets him constantly, of course, at Sir Walter's home. When she is observed tête-à-tête with him on a street in Bath, we may infer that a significant though disgraceful connection has been established (pp. 222–23, 228). In *Sense and Sensibility*, just as poor Edward Ferrars becomes attached to the unscrupulous Lucy Steele purely through living in her father's house, so his overconfident brother Robert takes up with her after a private interview designed to stop the girl from marrying Edward.

Austen's attitude toward sexual passion makes a strict division between the pursuit of a woman as an object of pleasure and the courtship of a lady whom one is to marry. When Scott, in *Redgauntlet*, describes Darsie Latimer as losing interest in the beautiful Lilias simply because she obeys her uncle's wish to kiss the young man, Scott does what Austen could not do: he treats courtship and the pursuit of pleasure as starting from the same impulse (chapter 18 of part 2). It is not that Austen ignored this common origin but that, being an undifferentiated appetite (like gluttony), it does not activate her system of moral coordinates. Only after the point of division between reverent courtship and licentious chase does the impulse have meaning for Austen.

Scott cannot handle moral implications, sexual passion, or courtship so subtly as Austen. The reason is that he is taken up with politics and religion. The conflicts inherent in such issues are so bold that they dominate his methods of characterization and capture the plots of his novels. In *Waverley*, for example, the entire childhood and education of the hero are designed to station him between Jacobitism and Whiggery. The course of the story then serves to place Waverley where the strains between the two sides will tug at him.

In *The Heart of Mid-Lothian*, the division between the old faith and the new overwhelms the portraits of Jeanie Deans, her father, and Reuben Butler. The novelist must plan his incidents and dialogue to exemplify this conflict. Even Jeanie's heroism becomes a tribute to the conscience of the saving remnant.

In *Rob Roy* none of the difficulties hindering the romance

between Diana Vernon and Frank Osbaldistone derive from the character of either. All are due to politics and religion. The personality of the villain Rashleigh is a caricature of the Gothic novelist's Jesuit. In portraying the heroine as a mysteriously inaccessible virgin huntress, Scott almost reduces her to an emblem of the goddess for which she is named, while her Roman Catholic faith places her, temporarily out of reach, in a nunnery.

Austen, who does not work with conventional symbols, must play down the issues that fascinate Scott if she is to liberate her genius. So it is that her clergymen, whether heroes or fools, never discuss doctrine. If they did so, by her scheme of moral, metonymic contrasts, she would have to treat one sect as superior to another, and the religious distinction would bury the individual traits. So also, as Gilbert Ryle has observed, the protagonists of Austen's novels face their moral crises without visible recourse to religious faith; nor do they ever seek the advice of a clergyman.[15]

For Austen, religion is a universal but indiscriminate context. She is not concerned to rank types of Christians any more than she ranks types of Englishmen. She chooses families that share the same region, the same church, the same social order— the same opportunities to strengthen their moral natures; and then she sees what the individuals make of themselves under these conditions.

It seems clear that Austen was reacting against sanctimoniousness. The strength of her own piety will be acknowledged by those who read with care the letters she wrote on her father's death, or her sister Cassandra's letters on Jane Austen's death. This impression is deepened by the admittedly protective *Memoir* written by her nephew J. E. Austen-Leigh. But living

---

15. "Jane Austen and the Moralists," in B. C. Southam, ed., *Critical Essays on Jane Austen* (London: Routledge and Kegan Paul, 1968), p. 117. Actually, Ryle is not quite right. Cf. Marianne's language in *Sense and Sensibility*, pp. 346–47, and Fanny's prayers and "solicitude" in *Mansfield Park*, pp. 264 and 428; also Fanny's use of "God grant," ibid., p. 424. Anne Elliot's advice clearly reflects her own practice, when she recommends "examples of moral and religious endurances" to Benwick (*Persuasion*, p. 101). I am indebted to Miss Carol Hinds for these references.

in a milieu in which overstatements of zeal were suspect, it was natural for her to look askance at the Evangelicals and to shrink from noisy expressions of spirituality.[16]

Nevertheless, by the quietest implications, Austen does establish something like a religious position in the novels. I do not refer to hints like Anne Elliot's distrust of her cousin for tolerating Sunday travel (*Persuasion*, p. 161), or even Edmund's speech in *Mansfield Park* on the powers of a clergyman (pp. 92–93), but to a far more general suggestion. This is the notion of rewards flowing from acts of kindness and charity. Now and then in the novels this principle delicately shows itself. Benevolent deeds become not only pleasures in themselves but also the mysterious causes of personal advantage.

In *Persuasion* the novelist early establishes the charitable disposition of her heroine.[17] When Anne goes to Bath, she feels sorry for an old schoolmate, Mrs. Smith, who is now a poor, widowed invalid. Anne goes regularly to comfort and entertain this obscure and isolated woman whose story is a negative analogue of her own.[18] Sir Walter and Elizabeth, the selfish father and sister, tease Anne for connecting herself with so mean an acquaintance. But Anne persists. And it is from Mrs. Smith that she then receives an autobiographical tale of the sort used by Fielding in *Tom Jones*.

Mrs. Smith not only illuminates the perils in Anne Elliot's path. She also gives her precious information that keeps her from any possibility of yielding to Mr. Elliot. Austen dwells on the link between goodness and its reward:

> She had never considered herself as entitled to reward for not slighting an old friend like Mrs. Smith, but here was a reward indeed springing from it!—Mrs. Smith had been able to tell her what no one else could have done.   (p. 212)

16. Chapman, *Jane Austen*, pp. 108, 114–15.

17. Anne tells her sister of the departure from Kellynch Hall: "And one thing I have had to do . . . going to almost every house in the parish, as a sort of take-leave. I was told that they wished it" (p. 39). One assumes that they wished it out of gratitude.

18. Paul N. Zietlow, "Luck and Fortuitous Circumstance in *Persuasion*," *ELH* 32 (1965): 134.

Perceptive critics have drawn attention to the large part played by coincidence and chance in the plot of *Persuasion*,[19] and one has observed that these elements traditionally suggest the interposition of Providence in the affairs of men.[20] I think his interpretation is borne out by the allusion to rewards in Anne Elliot's reflections on Mrs. Smith's providential exposure of Mr. Elliot. The whole course of the novel seems calculated to encourage us to trust in Providence. This is how I understand Anne Elliot's language when she goes over in her mind the melancholy decision she had once made to reject Wentworth's proposal. How eloquent, says Austen, "were her wishes on the side of early warm attachment, and a cheerful confidence in futurity, against that over-anxious caution which seems to insult exertion and distrust Providence!" (p. 30). When the lovers are securely reunited, Austen contrasts the fortunate Wentworth with the undeserving Sir Walter, who had failed "to maintain himself in the situation in which Providence had placed him" (p. 248).

Other touches evoke a framework of Christian doctrine, though not very audibly. The turning point of *Persuasion* is the scene on the Cobb at Lyme, when Louisa Musgrove, whom Wentworth has praised for her firmness, insists on being jumped down the stairs a second time but acts too hastily, misses his hands, and knocks herself unconscious upon the ground (p. 109). Louisa's fall reverberates forward and backward over the novel.

First, it recalls Austen's uncharacteristic use of metaphor during an earlier episode, in which Wentworth compared Louisa to an unspoiled hazelnut, beautiful and glossy when its brethren have been trodden under foot (p. 88). The moment faintly suggests the words of Christ, "Except a corn of wheat fall into the ground and die, it abideth alone: but if it die, it

19. Among others, Zietlow, cited above, and J. M. Duffy, "Structure and Idea in Jane Austen's *Persuasion*," *Nineteenth-Century Fiction* 8 (1954): 272–89.

20. Zietlow, p. 191.

bringeth forth much fruit" (John 12: 24). Louisa's firmness was of the wrong sort.[21]

Again, Austen recalls the fall in a superb scene near the end of *Persuasion*, after Anne Elliot has held forth to Captain Harville on the subject of fidelity. Having heard her outburst, Wentworth secretly conveys a letter to Anne, offering his love. Surrounded by three persons who witnessed the fall of Louisa (a fourth has just left), Anne is pressed between the need to hide the message and an impulse to exude some of the emotion that pervades her being. In her embarrassment she looks ill, and Louisa's mother feels anxious until assured repeatedly that "there had been no fall in the case" (pp. 235–38).

Austen seems to be relating the several scenes, drawing parallels between the firmness of whim and the firmness of devotion, or between Louisa's fall and Anne's exaltation, and giving the parallels a Christian aura; for Anne preferred conscience to self-indulgence and was rewarded (p. 246). I have no wish to impose allegory upon Austen's narrative design, or to make the religious overtone more than an evocation. But I think it is present.

Religion and morality join in Austen's broadest method of suggesting ethical principles, which is through the appointment of her characters and the shape of her plots. She had grown up with a choice of traditions in literature. On one side stood the humble domestic scenes of Richardson and Burney, the essays of Johnson, the poems of Cowper—all lighting up an ideal of lowly Christian heroism, opposed to the semipagan ideal of physical courage and chivalric honor. On the other side stood the tragic corruption of the pagan ideal, in the plot of *Clarissa*, the Gothic novel, the poems of Byron, and Scott's *Lord Marmion*.

In *Northanger Abbey* when Austen talks ironically about

21. Cf. Alistair Duckworth, *The Improvement of the Estate* (Baltimore: Johns Hopkins Press, 1971), p. 195. There may be a similar use of metaphor or allegory in the episode of the wilderness and gate in *Mansfield Park*, pp. 90–94, which perhaps alludes to Matthew 7: 13–14.

the concept of a heroine, she is not merely humorous. Through-out her novels she tries, as Mary Lascelles (her best critic) has said, to show that common life is finally more interesting, that it gives more nourishment to the healthy imagination, than the fantasies of romance.[22] This is of course the meaning of the scene in which Emma Woodhouse looks out from the doorway of a shop and fills her mind with the view of a village street (p. 233).[23] It is implied in Anne Elliot's great speech contrasting a woman's love with a man's (*Persuasion*, p. 235). It is embodied in the quiet, heroic endurance of Fanny Price, Elinor Dash-wood, and Anne Elliot herself.

The same principle appears in the vocations that Austen picked for her heroes: three clergymen, two country gentle-men, and only a single naval officer. Yet two of Austen's broth-ers became admirals, and her whole nation was at war for al-most two-thirds of her life. She had a minute familiarity with naval affairs and could have given an insider's view of battles at sea.

But Austen meant to domesticate the idea of a Christian hero. When Mr. Knightley, in *Emma*, dances with Harriet Smith to rescue her from Mr. Elton's scorn, he shows the cour-age that Austen wished to celebrate. When Tilney, in *North-anger Abbey*, defies his father and goes forth to find Catherine Morland, he is acting out Austen's response to the manners of the Giaour (pp. 247–48). It is no accident that Tilney is a parson while his arrogant father and frivolous brother follow military careers. In Austen's plots the turning points depend not on battles, duels, and hand-to-hand fights (as in Scott's novels) but on moral insights, on the sacrifice of ease not to glory but to duty: Elinor's ordeal of unexpressed misery in *Sense and Sensi-bility*, Fanny's resistance to Crawford in *Mansfield Park*.

Near the end of *Persuasion*, Austen has Wentworth wittily compare his experience of fortunate love to a heroic ordeal:

22. Mary Lascelles, *Jane Austen and Her Art* (Oxford: Clarendon Press, 1939), p. 71.
23. It is of course a mark of Emma's virtue that she does respond so favorably to the view.

> Like other great men under reverses ... I must endeavour to subdue my mind to fortune. I must learn to brook being happier than I deserve. (p. 247)

The remark is humorous, but the implication is serious: that the naval officer has endured a trial of character not through exposure to storms and bullets but through triumphing over a moral defect. By making such crises fascinating, Austen indicates how one may transform commonplace reality into an epic of the individual conscience.

Epilogue

A few years ago, I became uneasy about several approaches used by scholars and critics in dealing with literature of the period 1660–1760. So I tried to expose and analyze the errors which the practices led to.* What these interpreters shared, I thought, was an evasion of the explicit meanings of the works they examined.

But my own arguments were sometimes taken as suggesting that once a reader apprehended the explicit meaning of a poem, he knew all the poem had to offer. This of course was never my view. I decided therefore to articulate my true position by giving examples of justifiable or legitimate approaches to the evocative power of the literature sometimes called "Augustan."

One obstacle to the plan was the position occupied by the authors themselves. In expounding or defending their own works, they could sound as if they considered their meaning to be always simple and as if lucidity were their sole principle of style. One finds them recommending easy intelligibility as an overriding virtue, and objecting to ingenious (or not so ingenious) misinterpretations of their work. I have confronted this

Literary Meaning and Augustan Values (Charlottesville: University Press of Virginia, 1974).

obstacle in my introduction. In the rest of the book I have produced and analyzed many examples of the methods employed by lucid moralists to convey their meaning subtly and indirectly as well as explicitly.

Originally, I assumed that theories of implication, irony, allegory, etc., would be of central value in such an enterprise. Gradually, I learned that the historical context of the works contributed far more to one's understanding of them than any system of analysis. Reading the works over and over again, studying other works by their authors, comparing the primary texts with works by other authors, giving some consideration to sources, and—above all—striving to sympathize with the poet's individual processes of imagination and creation—such methods proved the most helpful. They transcend even the distinctions I expected to find among genres.

The dangers to be avoided were two: the substitution of information about the works for the direct experience of them, and a failure to keep in mind the need to judge the works, to consider their literary value at the same time as their meaning. I have tried to indicate why Dryden's serious plays hold and fascinate me, why *The Drapier's Letters*, though rougher in texture, seem a greater achievement than *The Examiner*, why Pope is always worth minute study, and why Austen remains a supreme literary artist at the same time as she is an obtrusive moralist. In all these projects I have taken the explicit meaning into account although normally going beyond it.

Index